Europe Day

Hartmut Marhold

Europe Day
How European Integration Got Started

PETER LANG

Bibliographic Information published by the
Deutsche Nationalbibliothek
The Deutsche Nationalbibliothek lists this publication in the Deutsche
Nationalbibliografie; detailed bibliographic data is available online at
http://dnb.d-nb.de.

Library of Congress Cataloging-in-Publication Data
A CIP catalog record for this book has been applied for at the
Library of Congress.

The English translation of this book has been supported by the Jean Monnet
Foundation for Europe. And: This book was first published 2020 in German by
Tectum, under the title Europatag. Wie Europas Einigung ihren Anfang nahm.
The translation into English has been revised by Deborah Kershaw

ISBN 978-3-631-88464-5 (Print)
E-ISBN 978-3-631-88481-2 (E-PDF)
E-ISBN 978-3-631-88482-9 (EPUB)
10.3726/b19972

© Peter Lang GmbH
Internationaler Verlag der Wissenschaften
Berlin 2022
All rights reserved.

Peter Lang – Berlin · Bern · Bruxelles · New York · Oxford · Warszawa · Wien

All parts of this publication are protected by copyright. Any
utilisation outside the strict limits of the copyright law, without
the permission of the publisher, is forbidden and liable to
prosecution. This applies in particular to reproductions,
translations, microfilming, and storage and processing in
electronic retrieval systems.

This publication has been peer reviewed.

www.peterlang.com

Table of contents

Part 1 People and events 7

    I Jean Monnet, the inventor and his plan (14–28 April 1950) 9

    II Robert Schuman – the plan enters the political stage (1 to 8 May) 29

    III Europe Day 49

    IV The controversy on 9 May 65

    V Schuman's speech 93

    VI After 9 May 99

Part 2 Rethinking the Schuman plan 105

    I Blocs versus continent? External (extra-European) and intra-European motives for integration 109

    II Economics or politics? Was the launch of European integration more an economic move or was it motivated by political objectives? 119

III Management or politics? Was the European Coal and Steel Community a project for pragmatic market management or a genuine political project? 127

IV Federation or international organization? What kind of political system is the European Community/Union? 135

V Interests or values? Was European integration more marked by shared values or was it about balancing interests? 143

VI Structures and people "Were structural constraints or the free choice of individuals decisive for the path towards European integration?" 149

Conclusions
European integration then and now 155

Part 1 People and events

I Jean Monnet, the inventor and his plan (14–28 April 1950)

Paris, East-Station, in a hurry ...

Friday afternoon, 28 April 1950. At the Gare de l'Est in Paris, the crowd pushes on the platforms. They want to leave the city, spend the weekend at home. There were already many commuters at the time, in particular here in Paris – "Paris and the French Desert" is the title of a bestseller, which denounced, three years before, the extent to which the whole of France was designed to serve Paris, how the capital devoured all available resources, how the "province" was neglected. And there were not yet so many individual cars. The Parisian dead-end stations distributed the commuters to all directions towards home: From the Gare de l'Est, the trains left heading to Reims and beyond, to Lorraine, its capital Metz and further on.[1]

The train to Metz is finally ready for boarding, many passengers push each other into the overcrowded coaches. At the same moment a man arrives on the platform, hastily, middle-aged, very correctly clothed, a briefcase under his arm, apparently in a hurry; he looks around, searching for somebody about to leave with this train, does not find him on the platform, gets more and more stressed, boards the train himself – and finally finds the one he was so urgently looking for. In a great haste, he hands the briefcase over to the other man, urging him: "Please read this during the weekend! It is really important and could be the solution for all our problems!" Then he has just the time to leave, the train is set in motion, the traveler is on the way home with the dossier at his disposal.[2]

---

1 The relationship between the French capital and the "province" was already at the time a big problem – in favour of the capital which sucked up all resources far and wide. See Jean-Jacques Gravier: Paris et le désert français. Paris 1947, many editions – the title tells the essential message.
2 The story told in this chapter follows the memoirs of Jean Monnet: Mémoirs. Paris 1976, p. 433. Most of the quotations have been translated for this book by its author.

10   Jean Monnet, the inventor and his plan (14–28 April 1950)

Who was the man on the platform? Who was the traveler? The hurrying searcher was Bernard Clappier, Chef de cabinet of the Foreign Minister, a high-ranking civil servant of the French Foreign Ministry, the 'Quay d'Orsay', as this prestigious seat of the French diplomacy is named after its location on the banks of the Seine river. And the man in the train was nobody else than the Minister himself, Robert Schuman, who usually took the train, modestly, as other commuters did, to get back to his hometown, Metz, and continued with a public bus to the small village at the outskirts of Metz, with the difficult name Scy-les-Chazelles, only 4 km away from the city centre, today integrated in the urban space of the Lorraine capital.

But why was it so urgent for Clappier to reach the Minister before the weekend before he left Paris? And what was the problem, which needed a solution at any rate and immediately? And what was this solution, which was apparently outlined in the dossier?

Pressure on France: Fix the German problem!

In those days, France found itself under heavy pressure – because of Germany. There was another meeting of the Foreign Ministers of the USA, the United Kingdom and France scheduled in London, from 10 May on, for a couple of days, and is was then that the French should finally commit themselves: What should be the future the newly founded West-German state, the Federal Republic of Germany would be allowed to envisage? Five years after the end of the war, the Germans were still the enemies in the eyes of most of the French, more than this: "hereditary enemies", that is enemies by nature, forever. The French interest was unambiguous, for many French, it could only be to hold the new West-German state down, as powerless as possible, at best even split it into its regional components, the "Länder", avoid any centralization of German power, at least control it tightly. To that purpose, the German industrial production, in particular in the West-German industrial powerhouse, the Ruhr region, should be limited to its minimum, in order to avoid the revival of the old conflicts over raw materials and resources, and that meant at the time for the industrialized West-European states coal and steel. The Germans should not be empowered to rebuild a predominant industry, France would prove to be unable to compete with; Germany should not gain sovereignty again over the resources which would enable et to lay the ground for renewed military construction.

It was decisive under these conditions to maintain control over the Ruhr region (and the Saarland), the by far most important reservoir of German industrial power nationwide. The German production in the Ruhr region should continue to be low and limited, the production quota should be tightly controlled, the Saar could and should be integrated in the French economic space altogether. On the whole, the French politics towards Germany was not profoundly different from what it was after the First World War – the 'solution' for the German problem should be to hold the new state powerless via stipulations and control mechanisms. No wonder then that this Frence politics was very unpopular, no wonder that the relations between the German chancellor, 74 years old Konrad Adenauer, and his French colleague – Robert Schuman – were frosty.

That was very different from the relations, which (West-)Germany had developed, in the meantime with the United States (and, to a lesser extent, with the United Kingdom). These two other Western allies perceived the situation in an altogether different way: The war coalition had long since been broken apart, the cleavage did no longer run between the Soviet Union, the United States, the United Kingdom (and France, as a junior partner) on the one hand and Nazi-Germany on the other; it was now the "Iron Curtain", as Winston Churchill hat dubbed the frontier between East and West. A new global antagonism had emerged, where the two new "Superpowers" were the poles, which put a spell on the whole world. The Marshall Plan in 1947, the Soviet blockade of Berlin in and the communist Putsch in Czechoslovakia in 1948, and the foundation of NATO in 1949 were milestones on the way to the formation of the "blocks". The West war now more frightened by the potential expansionism of Soviet communism than by a revival of a Nazi movement. Therefore, the USA (and, for different motives, the United Kingdom) had encouraged and supported the creation of a west-German state; it should assume its role in the defense against Soviet imperialism, as a member of the family of Western democracies. At the end of 1949, the West-Germans had become allies, in the eyes of the Americans, allies, which should be strengthened and eventually even entrusted with new weapons, so that their force would fortify the "free world". At any rate, the young Federal Republic should be allowed to rebuild its industry, and that would mean first of all: lift all the restrictions and controls imposed on West-Germany, those in particular which had weakened the German access to the natural resources of the Ruhr region, i.e. coal, the energy basis of nearly all industrial activity at the time. A flourishing German industry alone, even without armament, would be, in the perception of the Americans, a crucial contribution to the strengthening of the Western block, a strong asset to its resilience … and, last not least, indispensable as well for the American exports, which required a flourishing European consumer market.

… a horror scenario in the eyes of the French! That was self-evident, as well for the two Anglo-Saxon winners of the war: It was really difficult for France to align with this U-turn in their German politics. The USA and the United Kingdom, to some extent, understood the French fears vis-à-vis Germany. They were ready to let the French find a solution for the German question – but a solution had to be found, otherwise the two dominating Western powers would implement their own plan, and that would mean to liberate West-German industrial production from any constraints and in the medium term even the rearmament of the former enemy.

10th of May, in London, at the next conference of the foreign ministers, was the deadline: then, at the latest, France had to offer a solution. But two weeks ahead of this crucial date, end of April, the French government had not the slightest idea of what to do! They were simply lacking an idea of how to resolve the dilemma. Robert Schuman was literally haunted by the request of the Americans and the British to offer a solution for the German problem. That is the reason why Bernard Clappier was so much in a hurry to reach Robert Schuman that Friday afternoon, before the weekend, in the train towards Metz …

The Prime Minister is silent – Monnet and Clappier talk to each other

… for indeed, in his briefcase, he had the idea, which was so urgently needed to solve the German problem: the plan for a "European Community for Coal and Steel".

Bernard Clappier had just left the office of Jean Monnet, Rue de Martignac, only some hundred meters away from "The Quay d'Orsay", siege of the French Ministry of Foreign Affairs; the two men often met informally after the end of a laborious week, on Friday afternoons, when the Minister had left for the weekend. They knew each other well, appreciated their opinions mutually, trusted each other and used the relaxing moments at the beginning of the weekend to exchange their views on international relations and the rumors inside the French ruling class. This time, inevitably, their chat ended up with the upcoming conference of the Western Foreign Ministers in London, and Clappier did not conceal his anxiety – since there was no plan available, which could serve the French interest and at the same time satisfy the two other Western allies. Jean Monnet reminded Clappier of an earlier talk they had, two weeks before, when Monnet had already given some hints to a way in which he could imagine to tackle the problem, that Clappier wanted to talk to the Foreign Minister about those ideas, but that there was no feed-back since then.

Now, today, 28 of April, Monnet said, had he forwarded his ideas, now elaborated into a ful-fledged plan, to the Prime Minister, Georges Bidault, that is, more precisely to his closest collaborator, Falaize, asking for a meeting the next day, a request left without any reaction. Later, there were three competing explanations, which would explain the silence of Bidault ... we shall come back to this question.

Anyway, that Friday afternoon Bernard Clappier asked Jean Monnet whether he would allow him to have a look on this plan, which he himself had lost out of sight and memory and which the Prime Minister apparently did not take notice of. Monnet, sure that he had done his duty to inform the Prime Minister first, did not oppose himself, and Clappier got more and more excited and nervous when reading the short four pages of the plan – it was immediately obvious to him that this plan comprised the longed-for solution of the German question, the answer to the request of the other Western allies! Impassioned, Clappier asked Monnet whether he would allow him to hand this plan over to Robert Schuman, as quickly as possible, immediately, before the weekend – he believed that he still had a chance to join Schuman at the Gare de l'Est. Jean Monnet had no objections, on the contrary, this might be the last chance to open the way for the plan to enter the political arena. Clappier hurried away ...

But did this really happen in such a dramatic way? Did the destiny of the plan to launch the first European Community really depend on several minutes on the platforms of the Paris East Train Station? Indeed – as at other moments of this story –, there are competing versions of the succession of events, and sometimes the most scrupulous investigation cannot elucidate which the "right" version is. The version I offered above follows largely the memories of Jean Monnet, and the only other witness in this precise situation is Bernard Clappier. He described it in a more relaxed way, in an interview thirty years later. First of all, he confirms that he got to know the plan during a talk in Jean Monnets office that Friday afternoon, 8th of April, and then continues: "The same day, I handed the document over to Robert Schuman who was just about the leave Paris and to spend the weekend in his home at Scy-Chazelles in Lorraine. The Minister took the document with him in order to analyse it in tranquility." So far no divergence between the two accounts – but then Clappier adds: "When I took him to the East Train Station on *29th of April* [!], he just had read the paper and said to approximately this [...]"[3] There is no definite guarantee whether Jean Monnet or Bernard Clappier are more precise in their account of that moment, but the Memoirs of Monnet seem to be more trustable, more detailed, and more carefully elaborated then the oral interview Clappier gave thirty years after the event, hands-on, and which reveals the his own narrative is contradictory in itself, when he talks about Schuman's intention to leave Paris on Friday afternoon – on the one hand – and his being still present the next day – on the other hand.

Obviously, the question arises whether Schuman himself holds the answer and whether he communicated it. The answer to this question

---

3 The original French version reads as follows: "Ce que je viens de vous raconter se passait le vendredi 28 avril 1950. Je remis ce jour-là la note de Jean Monnet à Robert Schuman qui était sur le point de quitter Paris pour aller passer la fin de la semaine chez lui à Scy-Chazelles en Lorraine. Le ministre emporta donc le document pour pouvoir l'étudier tranquillement. Lorsque je l'accompagnais gare de l'Est, le 29 avril, ayant lu rapidement la note de Monnet, il me dit à peu près ceci [...]". Interview with Bernard Clappier: Auszüge über die Ursprünge des Schuman-Plans und die Rolle Jean Monnets (11. November 1980); in: *L'Europe une longue marche*. Lausanne: Fondation Jean Monnet pour l'Europe, Centre de recherches européennes, 1985, pp. 20–26. Available online: http://www.ena.lu/interview_bernard_clappier_auszuge_uber_ur- sprunge_schuman_ plans_rolle_ jean_monnets_november_1980–3-35994.

is somewhat disappointing for historians and all interested readers who want to be sure about the story and wish for an accurate reconstruction of the facts – it is at the same time honourable for Schuman himself: The man was simply too modest to write an autobiography or any other form of memoirs. He did not consider himself as important enough, he felt that he "would not deserve the interest of any reader".[4] And his personal archives are not carefully gathered and stored, filed, archived, they are dispersed and sometimes untraceable. Schuman considered is as much more important to deliver his convictions about Europe than to write his life: "Pour l'Europe", "For Europe" is the title of the slim, but very substantial booklet, where he relates and justifies his engagement for peace, welfare and Franco-German reconciliation. The by far most reliable source for the events of those days still are and will be the memoirs of Jean Monnet.[5]

The author of the plan: Cognac and business

Supposed it was really as exciting as Jean Monnet remembers it – how comes that it was just him who imagined such a plan, him who was not at all mandated to do so? Jean Monnet was a particularly interesting, a curious man, a man who was not really a politician and never wanted it to become, and who nevertheless had such huge influence on French and even international politics. Monnet's office, Rue de Martignac, located at one edge of a triangle between the Palais Bourbon, siege of the French Prime Minister, the Foreign Office, on the Quai d'Orsay, was the headquarter of a unique administration, the "Commissariat au Plan", the planning agency for the French economy. A planning agency – for a market, not communist, economy?! Indeed, their task was economic planning, with the specific feature that the five years plans put forward by this agency were not binding, but recommendations for politicians and managers, it was not a command structure like in the countries under Soviet hegemony. Still, these five years plans had an impact on allocating investment, the

---

4 Robert Schuman: Pour l'Europe. Paris 1964 (2. edition), p. 12.
5 Concerning the question of the reliability of Jean Monnet's memoirs see: Delphine Pandazis: Jean Monnet et ses mémoires: Les coulisses d'une longue entreprise collective. Paris 2018.

French state assumed the role of a steering agency for the economy, indicating objectives and ways to reach them, fully in line with the French understanding of statehood (influential until today), as an incarnation of the "volonté Générale", the national interest in its absolute form.

Jean Monnet was well qualified to assume the function of the president of this planning agency. A short look on his biography is more than an anecdotical divertissement, but contributes largely to understanding the project, which would become a birth certificate of European integration. Born in 1888 in the city of Cognac, he was the son of a family, which cultivated – and still does cultivate – Cognac[6], a cultural and artisanal heritage in the South-West of France. A large share of the production in this region, including Bordeaux wines, are traditionally exported to Anglo-Saxon countries. To this purpose, Jean Monnet was sent to the United States and Canada already as a young man, before the first World War, mandated to negotiate with commercial partners the price of his family's Cognac. This provided him with the opportunity to learn English (rather exceptional in France, at that moment of history!), but to become acquainted with the business practice, the way to broke "deals", the mentality of the Americans, sometimes during adventurous rides on horseback across the hardly populated regions far away from the Atlantic coast. Trust becomes a fundamental value for him, who learns and knows that he can attach his pony to the fence of a farm for a couple of days and find it unscathed at the same place.

During the First World War, Jean Monnet enrolls in the French army, but not as a soldier – he serves his country in a more unusual way. The still young man offers his services in the field of logistics, he is charged with the supply of the French and the British armies fighting side by side at the same front, in the North of France, against the Germans. The task fails to make him desperate, because the politicians and generals of both countries consider the needs of their respective armies, on behalf of national sovereignty, as top secret, an attitude which prevents Monnet from getting the information he needs in order to mobilise the appropriate resources. He himself would privilege nothing else than the pragmatic, the best adapted

---

6 See http://monnet-cognac.com/fr/accueil/.

The author of the plan: Cognac and business   17

solution for the common duty, whereas national pride and mistrust, considerations of sovereignty and glory of the participating actors seem to him irrelevant. His experience with this situation would become crucial for his later role in the foundation of the European Communities: Motivations of the politicians, aiming at the defense and maintenance of sovereignty of their nation states, personal glory and party politics, public and electoral recognition are all more or less superfluent and counterproductive for the solution of real problems. Their solution should be conferred upon experts, who act in a pragmatic key, simply straightforward to the solution, guided by expertise and knowledge-based analysis and not by the abstract ideology of the sovereign nation state.

After the First World War, Monnet served the League of Nations, as Deputy Secretary General. But here again, he was disappointed and disillusioned by the factionalism among the member states and their political self-definition, it was again sacred cow of "Sovereignty", which stood in the way of common decisions. The lesson he drew from this experience was: If sovereignty is required among a set of sovereign states, as a necessary condition for common decision, then there will simply be no common decision. Monnet returned to business, founded a bank in China, revived his relations with American business partners – and still got back to the political arena in the Second World War: What was now at stake was existential. As special envoy of the British (!) government, he contributed, between 1940 and 1943, to convince the Roosevelt administration, and the President personally, that the dimension of the war efforts had to be doubled up for final victory. From Washington he found his way to the French exile government of General de Gaulle and participated in his provisional government in Algers, already then by elaborating a plan for a transnational, federal Europe based on a common economy. In 1943, he laid his views down in a still very modern, topic memorandum: "There will be no peace in Europe as long as the recovery of the states will be based again on the principle of national sovereignty, which will inevitably entail politics aiming at reputation and standing and economic protectionism. [...] The nation states of Europe are too small to provide their populations with the prosperity, which modern conditions allow for and therefore require. They need bigger markets. [...] Their prosperity and social evolutions are impossible unless the European states form a federation or a 'European

Authority', which would shape an economic unity."⁷ Jean Monnet was always able and willing to imagine the big picture, he was aware of the global scope of the new era. There was no doubt that he would be part of the leading elite in post-war France, despite being no politician. And there was no doubt neither that he would have a specific, pragmatic, solution-oriented look on the political situation.

Five years after the War – what about Europe?

And the political situation had become dangerous – or was still dangerous since the end of the War. The two powers, elevated to "Super-"powers after the War, no longer stood side by side against a common enemy, but faced each other as more and more unreconcilable antagonists, as enemies. The formation of NATO, in 1949, was the last step on the way to the emergence of the "Blocks", which would shape global politics for nearly half a century and make the globe a "bi-polar" world, with one pole in Moscow and the other in Washington.

And Europe? The Eastern part of the continent, starting just in the middle, in its heart, right through Germany, dividing its capital Berlin, was irretrievably lost, as it seemed, surrendered to the Soviet sphere of power. And Stalin, the Soviet dictator, had left no doubt, what that meant. In April 1945 he had put in in these words, talking to the Yugoslav resistant Milovan Djilas: "This war is not as in the past. Whoever occupies a territory also imposes on it his own social system. Everyone imposes his own system as far as his army can reach. It cannot be otherwise. If now there is not a communist government in Paris, this is only because Russia has no an army which can reach Paris in 1945."⁸ But the West had to play its role as well and the United States left no doubt that they insisted on everybody assuming his function. Sure, their influence had nothing in

---

7   Jean Monnet: Memorandum as of 5ᵗʰ August 1943, Algiers; quoted from: https://www.cvce.eu/content/publication/1997/10/13/b61a8924-57bf-4890-9e4b-73bf4d882549/publishable_de.pdf.
8   Quoted many times, here from: https://digitalarchive.wilsoncenter.org/resource/cold-war-history/joseph-stalin; originally in Milovan Djilas: Conversations with Stalin. Harcourt 1962.

common with the brutal hegemony of the Soviet Union – the best example for the difference is the Marshall Plan. It was designed to get the West European economies under steam again, by means of market and competition of course, but supported by cooperation beyond borders among the aid receiving countries, if possible even by transnational federalization. Under these conditions the Americans were ready to put huge sums for investment at the otherwise free disposal of the Europeans, up to 3% of their national GDP.

Within Europe, movements popped up which aimed at preserving the independence of the continent and at the same time at overcoming the old conflicts between the European nation states. Former members of the resistance movements in particular, of many European countries, had found a common ground in their new engagement for Europe, for a European Union, a European Federation, for the United States of Europe. This new European political community, whatever be the exact shape and name, should exactly deliver this: solve the internal, intra-European conflicts between its nations peacefully and – externally – safeguard the independence of Europe.[9]

These "Euro-federalists" were, at their own surprise, hugely encouraged, supported and fueled by a highly esteemed statesmen, indeed probably the most prestigious statesmen after the Second World War in Europe: Winston Churchill. As early as in September 1946 did he launch his idea of the "United States of Europe", in a famous speech delivered at the University of Zurich, addressing the "academic youth of Europe", emphasizing the need to "start now"! However, and that was the grief of the continentals, these "United States" would only be those of the continent – whereas the United Kingdom would be among its "friends and sponsors", at the same rank as the USA and, as Churchill hoped for, the Soviet Union. This project triggered a large civil society movement, the "European Movement", which should, notwithstanding all divergencies, launch the process of uniting Europe.

---

9   See the Hertenstein Programme on the website of Federal Union: https://federalunion.org.uk/the-hertenstein-programme/.

20   Jean Monnet, the inventor and his plan (14–28 April 1950)

The first big meeting of the European Movement, the Congress of the Hague, from 8 to 10 May 1948, in the Dutch capital, was meant to hand the project over from civil society to the political arena, to those who should feel obliged to implement it. Churchill threw all his weight into the balance, but the cleavages were unbridgeable and weakened the message decisively: Should the destroyed and powerless states on the continent really do the crucial step towards unification and leave outside the only surviving power of global relevance, the United Kingdom? Should sovereignty really be transferred to a European Union, i.e. should Europe go the way towards a federal unity, or should the nation states stay sovereign and form only a looser (con-)federal union? And should the Europeans take this critical step right now, in a moment, when the Soviet Union prevented the Central Europeans to go along with their Western counterparts – shouldn't the Europeans wait for a more propitious moment, try to convince the Soviet Union that such a Union would not endanger their legitimate desire for granted security, but serve it?

The outcome of the Congress was meager, but in the short run it could be interpreted as heading in the right direction: Just one year after the Congress, 5th May 1949, the Council of Europe was founded in Strasbourg – Churchill hat already mentioned such a thing in his speech in Zurich, three years and a half earlier, as a "first step". But was this really the first step on the to the United States of Europe? For some time still after its foundation, the Council of Europe was credited to become the "engine" of European unification, but relatively soon it became clear that this new international organization would not live up to its ambitions. One of the problems which overshadowed the Congress of the Hague had been solved: The United Kingdom was a founding member of the Council of Europe. But it was just this achievement, which disabled the Council to go for a transfer of sovereignty, because the United Kingdom itself was entirely hostile to any such further step. The Council of Europe got stuck in this dilemma, its decisions were not binding for the member states, his power way hypothetical.

That became obvious in the eyes of the most impatient and engaged actors in the institutional setting of the Council of Europe, i.e. the delegates from national parliaments, which formed the Parliamentary Assembly of the Council. During the first period of its meetings, in winter 1949-1950, they discussed sometimes very emphatically all imaginable options for the further development of their Council into a European federal system – and had to recognize that Europe in fact needed just the opposite of what the European Council was. Whereas its competences were very large, nearly unlimited, including all policy fields – the only exception were security issues, reserved for NATO –, the Council of Europe had no real power to take and much less implement any decision: Unanimity in the decisive institution, the Committee of Ministers, was the obstacle, preserving national sovereignty, most often on the insistence of the United Kingdom. The delegates in the Parliamentary Assembly, desperate about their powerlessness, developed a formula, which was the precise alternative to what they lived: What Europe needed was a real political authority, mandated with the power to take binding decisions; on the other hand (at least in the short run), this critical power should be limited to some few, carefully chosen, precisely delimited policies – only then would such a supranational institution be acceptable for the nation states, safeguarding jealously their sovereignty.[10] Jean Monnet's plan met exactly the contours of this design, it was the perfect translation of the formula into a pragmatic project.

Coal does not know national borders – Jean Monnet's idea

Jean Monnet was perfectly adapted to the function he had to assume as president of the French planning agency. His experience as entrepreneur, his neutral expertise, his capacity to analyse and organize were extremely precious for his tasks. Early in the year 1950, he too was aware that the German question had become the most urgent problem for France's diplomacy. But he was aware of more than that: With his team he looked into a future where the French industry, and namely the coal and steel industry in the north of France, would no longer be competitive at international level, most of all with the German corporations of the Ruhr region. The French structures were too outdated, the milieu of the French entrepreneurs was to hostile to innovation, the resources were too limited, especially just

---

10 See Heinrich Schneider: Leitbilder der europäischen Integration 1 – Der Weg zur Integration. Bonn 1976.

those of coal and steel. Jean Monnet, largely free from considerations regarding national sovereignty, was able to have a look on the map of Europe without prejudice, on a map showing the deposits of coal, a map where the borders between the nation states played only a secondary role. Such a map reveals the evidence, unfortunately for the nation states, that coal, below their soil, shows no respect for national border lines – it lies deep in the earth under Northern France, Southern Belgium, Luxembourg, the region of the Saar and, in great quantities, in the West German Ruhr region. One only had to put the whole of this large European transborder region, with all their coal and together with the steel industry, under a common administration. This would serve several purposes at the same time:

First of all, it would create a great pool, a great market, a great reservoir of the main energy resources, where all the companies would compete under common regulations, wherever they might be located – in France, Germany, Belgium, Luxembourg. Such a common market would provide the French companies with access to the whole of the coal region, instead of being limited to the smaller share of what could be found under French territory. At the same time, the French companies would be exposed to a mobilizing competition, would awake them from their lethargy and oblige them to finally go for modernization and innovation.

Second, such a supranational agency for coal and steel would withdraw from the states – an in particular from the new West German one – the authority over those so important resources and lift it to a superior, "supranational" level, a European one. Withdraw the authority over coal and steel would mean to deprive them of these existential economic sectors as means of power politics. Conflicts between the participating states would be literally, materially excluded, if coal and steel would be no longer state bound industries. And, most important, no participating state would dispose any longer of the means to prepare a new war, since the resources would be under a common control. The establishment of a community for coal and steel would be a decisive step towards peace keeping, in particular between France and Germany of course. Instead of uncontrolled concurrence between the two "hereditary enemies", there would emerge a regulated competition between companies of all member states, based on common rules, common legislation. In such an ensemble the deeper causes for war bound conflicts would be unrooted and any preparation of war rendered impossible.

And, last not least, such a supranational organization, even if it required a transfer of sovereignty, would just stay beyond the limit of what was acceptable for nation states jealous of their status as sovereign states. In the end, at stake were "only" two sectors of the economy, not the core of national sovereignty, like foreign or security policy. The step would not be perceived as a revolution – as the creation of the "United States of Europe" would have been; the participating states could continue to believe in their sovereignty.

Alpe d'Huez, conception place of Europe

Jean Monnet had turned around these ideas and looked at them from all side, until they were mature enough, in his personal, very specific method. He usually got off early in the morning but sat down at his office only at ten a.m. – every morning, he went out for a small hike in nature, far from the city, lost to the flow of his thoughts and ideas without too much directing them at will, listening to the sound of nature, open to the views of forest and field, then gathered his senses again, started to concentrate on what lay ahead, disentangled the important from the marginal, found solutions ... When spring came in 1950, he felt that even this method of looking at the duties from some distance was no longer enough to master his problems, he got out of office for two weeks, took the train to the Alpes, to Savoy, to the Alpe d'Huez, which friends of the Tour de France may know well as one of the most dramatic stages. "I do not remember how many kilometers we were walking in those two weeks, from refuge to refuge, but I still have the notes in mind, which I put on paper in the evenings when we were recovering."[11] It is here that his plan took shape – the first European Community was conceived at the Alpe d'Huez.

Back in Paris, he became aware that he needed experts to substantiate his ideas – lawyers for the legal, constitutional architecture, economists for the economic aspects. 14th April, another Friday, two weeks ahead of the decisive meeting with Bernard Clappier, he met with Paul Reuter,

---

11 Monnet, Mémoires, a.a.O., S. 416.

law professor at the renowned university of Aix-en-Provence, who was external advisor to the French Ministry of Justice. Monnet took the opportunity to explain to Reuter – born in Lorraine, as Schuman, and therefore supposedly receptive for Franco-German relations – in short words what he was trying to figure out. Reuter was immediately enthusiastic, so much so, that Monnet asked him to come back the next day and dive into the details of the whole project. Both men spent most of that Saturday, 15th April, together, working on the draft plan, and invited for Sunday, 16th April, another intimate and collaborator of Jean Monnet at the planning agency, Etienne Hirsch. This was the day, which ended with the first written version of what would become, three weeks later, the "Schuman plan". However, this draft version is marked not 16th, but 17th April – understandably, because the small working group hat met at Houjarray, close to Montfort-l'Amoury, Monnet's private property[12] (from 1945 through to his death in 1979), around 50 kilometers south-west of Paris, and there was no secretary – Madame Suzanne Miguez, his longstanding secretary in office, could typewrite the text only the next Monday, 17th April.[13] The same day, Monnet invited Pierre Uri[14] to join the task force – a newcomer in his team, which is now stuffed enough with experts to allow for a sort of division of labor: Uri looks at the economic aspects, Reuter at the institutional ones.

"Over the next days, there were various other versions, which could be interpreted as stages of our reflection", writes Monnet in his memoirs[15], and indeed there were two, not precisely dated versions, probably due to the participation of Uri since that Monday, 17th April. From the second version on, the text is structured into chapters (five on the whole, with Latin figures), seemingly the work of the newly initiated Uri: "He contributed

---

12 Monnet lived there from 1945 to his death in 1979; his house is today a memorial open to the public.
13 Monnet mentions „Mme Miguez" only once in his memoirs, as „ma fidèle secrétaire", his „devoted secretary" – her first name occurs only in the index, not in the text, and Monnet does not count her among the "initiates" ...
14 Pierre Uri, much younger, born in 1911, was economist, academic and political advisor, most often in socialist governments, until the Mitterand era in the 80s.
15 Monnet, Mémoires, op.cit, p. 427; see further comments there on the versions of the plan and the changes which occurred.

essentially. The text became better structured, the institutional system was spelled out more accurately: The International Authority ["Autorité internationale"] became the High Authority ["Haute Autorité commune", in the French original]."[16] Both of these improvements – structuring and terminology for the institutions – can be assigned to both of the two collaborators: structuring is Uri's work (from the second version on), the terminology of the institutional setting is Reuter's (from the third version on). "Anyway, Reuter was the inventor of the High Authority, in terms and in substance".[17] This "High Authority" is nothing else than the present European Commission. Its present name goes back to the Rome Treaties of 1957, but its birthday can be precisely fixed to Monday, 17th April 1950, Paul Reuter was its "midwife", and the birth certificate was the third version of what at that moment still was a Monnet Plan, becoming the Schuman plan only three weeks later.

Monnet could bring his colleagues to the point of despair with his obsession to overhaul a text again and again – as he did this time, before version number 9 would become the final one. "Nine versions came after one another between Sunday, 16th April, and Saturday, 6th May. I cannot say, whether this is many or a few versions – in such a situation, I do not follow any other rule than to work on it as much as is needed, a hundred times with commitment, if a hundred times is needed, until I am satisfied with the result, or nine times, as in this case, most often fifteen times, would my former collaborators say, who would have been easily satisfied with less. The proof is, as the say: In the end, we usually come back to the first version, which has proved to be the best one. [This was different this time!] But what tells us such a balance sheet of efforts? How can you know that the first version is the best one, if you did not compare it with others, which could have been better? As if everything was alright, when you trust

---

16 „Uri contribuerait pour sa part avec bonheur. Le texte devint plus structuré, le systéme institutionnel s'affermit: L'Autorité internationale devint la Haute Autorité commune." Monnet, Mémoires, op.cit., p. 430.

17 Monnet, Mémoires, op.cit, p. 431. „Schuman et Clappier venaient d'entrer dans le cercle des conjurés où Bidault et Falaize ne les rejoignirent pas, er pour cause: Ils n'avaient pas pris le temps de lire ma lettre dans laquelle je demandais un rendez-vous pour le lendemain afin de commenter la proposition jointe".

exclusively in intuition and chance to lead you to the precise formulation of a thought, which still searches to become clear! At least, intuition and chance must be exposed to test – and that test is a renewed reading after a healthy sleep at night, or else a critical new look [of a new reader]."[18]

It took a couple of days, until the midst of next week, before the work on the text began again, but then came a very intense stage of elaboration: They revised the plan on Wednesday, Thursday and Friday, 26th, 27th and 28th April, but now Monnet decided to send the seventh version to the Prime Minister, George Bidault. He notes on a copy of this version with his own hand: "Version sent to Bidault, 28th April, Schuman, 2nd May, R. Mayer, 4th May."

And that is what happened: Friday afternoon, Monnet conveys this version of his plan to the head of office of the Prime Minister, Pierre-Louis Falaize, together with an explanatory note, asking for a personal meeting the next day. But this meeting did never come: Falaize and Bidault "did not take the time to read my letter", states Monnet in his memoirs.[19] Some moments after sending out the dossier to the office of the Prime Minister,

---

[18] The French original reads: „Neuf états se succédèrent entre le dimanche 16 avril et le samedi 6 mai. Je ne sais pas si c'est peu ou beaucoup – en cette matière, je n'ai d'autre règle que de travailler autant qu'il le faut, cent fois sur le métier si cent fois sont nécessaires pour que le résultat me donne satisfaction, ou neuf fois, comme dans cette circonstance, plus souvent quinze diront mes anciens collaborateurs qui se fussent volontiers contentés de moins. A preuve, disent-ils, nous revenions d'ordinaire à la première version qui se révélait être la meilleure. Mais que signifie cette comptabilité de l'effort? Comment être assuré que la première version est la meilleurs, sinon en la comparant à ce qu'on croît être meilleure encore? Que tout serait commode si l'intuition et le hasard conduisaient sans coup férir à l'exacte formulation d'une pensée qui n'aurait pas à se chercher! De moins, cette intuition et ce hasard demandent-ils à être mis à l'épreuve – et l'épreuve, c'est la relecture après une bonne nuit de sommeil ou la critique d'un regard neuf." Monnet, Mémoirs, op.cit, p. 429f.

[19] Clappier shares Monnet's opinion: „Georges Bidault, à mon avis, n'avait pas lu le papier que Falaize avait glissé dans un tiroir de son bureau." See the source available on the CVCE (Centre Virtuel de la Connaissance sur l'Europe, based in Luxembourg) webpage: http://www.cvce.eu/obj/interview_de_bernard_clappier_extraits_sur_les_origines_du_plan_schuman_et_le_role_de_jean_monnet_11_novembre_1980-fr-278699a3-a23a-4688-8fe2-c4a83186c762.html.

Clappier appears in Monnet's office and the initiative takes an altogether new direction.

Until this moment and besides Jean Monnet himself, only Paul Reuter, Etienne Hirsch, Pierre Uri and Bernard Clappier (in this temporal succession) were initiated to the plan (and, most often forgotten, Monnet's discreet, but best-informed secretary, Madame Miguez), that is five people. However, there were apparently at least two more how had gotten to know about the plan, outside the tight circle of intimates: Etienne Hirsch, high ranking collaborator of Jean Monnet in the planning agency, as already mentioned, and his successor in the function of president, was "the only one among the conspirators", according to his own words, "who had experiences in the industrial sector. [...] I asked Jean Monnet to allow me to consult one responsible in the coal, and one in the steel industry", bevor the plan would be open to the political and the public sphere. "Monnet agreed. As convened upon, I met with the President of the Association of Coal Industry, who was a member in our advisory committees, whom I knew very well and whom I could fully trust. I showed him the project and asked him what in his eyes would be the impact on the coal mining industry [...] He told me: 'Anyway, we have pits which are not competitive, especially in the South, but something has to be done anyway. You can do that.' As far as steel was concerned, the question was more complicated. I talked to a member of our committee on steel issues, whom I fully trusted. [...] His name war Aron [...] and his answer war: 'Either this or the death' [meaning that the French steel industry would not survive if the plan would not be implemented]. I was relieved."[20]

---

20 „C'est ça ou la mort". Extraits de l'interview d'Etienne Hirsch, ancien Commissaire général du Plan et Président d'Euratom, par Antoine Marès, à Paris, le 2 juillet 1980. In: Fondation Jean Monnet pour l'Europe (Hrsg.): L'Europe, une longue marche. S. 39f. Hirsch's man of confidence must have been Alexis Aron, see the obituary at the webpage of the French association of industrials: http://www.annales.org/archives/x/aron.html. See as well, along with a whole range of later academic articles, the short but authentic history of the French mining industry, written by its president, Philippe de Ladoucette: Charbonnages de France et la Société française, where he talks about the difficult implementation of Jean Monnet's plan aiming at an increase in production during the post-war years: http://annales.org/ri/2004/mai/ladoucette07-17.pdf; Annales des Mines,

One thing is for sure, the plan had took shape in those days, had been substantiated with expertise; but it was still a plan, known only to a handful of Jean Monnet's intimate friends and still without any perspective to become politically relevant, much less being implemented – Clappier had given no feedback since two weeks, it seemed that Schuman was not interested: Another misunderstanding, as became obvious that Friday, 28th April, wenn Clappier showed up again in Monnet's office.[21] It was circumstances, not lack of interest, which had hold back a reaction of the Minister, who wanted a written, elaborated project, not just a few vague words, and this and that had prevented Clappier to meet with Monnet for the last two weeks – and now everything got extremely urgent …

Mai 2004. The president of the mining association was probably Roger Cadel; see the list of the presidents here: https://fr.wikipedia.org/wiki/Charbonnages_de_France#Pr%C3%A9sidents-directeurs_g%C3%A9n%C3%A9raux.

21 Clappier remembers, although not exactly, this communication with Jean Monnet: „Un mois plus tard, c'était vers le 10 ou le 15 avril, Monnet m'interroge sur les réactions de R. Schuman. 'Que pense-t-il de tout cela, de mes projets?' Je lui réponds en lui faisant observer que je n'ai qu'une connaissance verbale de ses idées, et que mon patron aime les écrits, les textes qu'il peut étudier à loisir. C'est donc en lui remettant un texte qu'on pourra obtenir de lui une réaction sérieuse." See Footnote 19.

II Robert Schuman – the plan enters the political stage (1st to 8th May)

Lonely decision during weekend

On Monday, 1st of May, Robert Schuman, back from Scy-Chazelles, stepped down from the train at the East-Station, at the same place where Bernard Clappier had met him three days before, handing over to him the plan of Jean Monnet. Schuman's first words were: "I'll do it." ... the decision had been taken, the plan was about the become the Schuman-Plan.

But what did really happen with Schuman, so that he was ready for a U-turn in French German politics? The pressure, the constraint, the need to offer, 10th May, a solution of the German problem to the two other Western allies, the plausibility of the plan, the convincing arguments of Jean Monnet – sure, but is this enough to explain such a dramatic shift from all previous politics and their abrupt reorientation? For abandoning partially French sovereignty in favour of a partnership with the neighbour country, which had been for so long a deadly enemy, now on the basis of equal rights? For the revolutionary idea to create a common, legitimate political authority beyond the nation states, a "supra-national" community?

And it was indeed one man, one personality, who operated this U-turn, who took the decision, who pushed it through: Robert Schuman. He knew that he had to minimize its meaning in the face of a skeptical Prime Minister and other Ministers, that he had to hide it away from the diplomats of his own, the French Foreign Ministry, from Parliament and Party, from the French public and media – most of the French politicians of the moment would not have agreed upon the implementation of the plan, because it implied a loss of French sovereignty, because it demanded too much trust in the former "hereditary enemy".

It cannot only be the situation and the pragmatic plausibility of the Monnet's ideas, which triggered Schuman's decision – others would have acted differently in this situation. Who was then this man? What was different with him? Which were the convictions leading him the this lonely decision – during the weekend of 29 and 30 April 1950, when he was alone in his home in Scy-Chazelles cloes to Metz, with Jean Monnet's plan on his private desk?

Robert Schuman, Christian, Lorrainer, French, European

When Robert Schuman was born in Luxembourg, in 1886, he was German citizen – because his father was Lorrainer and Alsace-Lorraine was part of the German Reich, since 1871. His father was a farmer just at the border between Lorraine and Luxembourg, his mother Luxembourger from a small French-speaking town twelve kilometers away. However, his father had fought on the French side in the war of 1870/71, his sympathy was for the French, even if he now officially considered himself as a "Lorrainer" – to insist on his French identity was forbidden, to agree on a German identity he denied. Robert was educated in two languages, or three, if one considers Luxembourgish, a variant of the German dialect of "Moselfränkisch", as an own language. At school, there are officially two languages, French and German, even if Luxembourgish is the most spoken language among the pupils. The family moves to Luxembourg, where Robert first gets acquainted and impressed by the feeling of patriotism, of emotional attachment – and to Luxembourg! –, at the solemn moment when the new Grand Duke Adolf is hailed by the citizens upon his entry in the capital; Robert Schuman, fourteen years old, cheers him in the crowd.

His father dies early, Robert, the only child in the family, attaches himself closely to the mother, bound by an early awoken and actively encouraged, intense, life-long Christian-catholic faith. For the last year at school, before the (German) "Abitur", he moves to Metz, on his own resolution – apparently searching for his identity as a Lorrainer. Between 1904 and 1908 he studies law in Bonn, Munich, Berlin and Strasbourg, with a wide horizon for other fields of knowledge and culture, in particular for German literature and philosophy, for Goethe and Kant, Hegel and Nietzsche. Schuman enrolls in a student's society, the Görres-Gesellschaft, equally bound by catholic values and scientific ethos. After his examination as a lawyer in 1912, he settles down in Metz, two years before the First World War breaks out, which made Alsace and Lorrain French provinces again. In his new professional function, he does not limit his action to legal affairs, but engages in manyfold civil society activities, as we would say today – in education along the catholic social doctrine, as it took shape only shortly after he was born in the Encyclic "Rerum Novarum" (1889). The Pope of the time, Leo XII., had raised the question how to conduct a Christian, catholic life under the conditions of the emerging industrial mass society, in particular among the working class, he had launched the appeal to found Christian trade unions, engaged on the side of the exploited proletariat against Manchester capitalism. In Metz, Robert Schuman made these concerns his own, and he stuck to this commitment lifelong. He had never any political ambition and thanks to poor health (recognized already in 1908) he escaped from the need to wear the uniform of any of the warrying neighbour states, France or Germany.

Before the First World War, his personality had taken shape and standing: His individual identity was multifaceted and multifunctional, there was a local fundament close to the border between Lorraine and Luxembourg, where he had spent his childhood; there was a regional level, maybe the strongest contribution to his personality, his attachment to Lorraine; it is difficult to assess correctly the national level of identity he felt, consciously or unconsciously, but he very probably did not feel "German"; to be a Frenchman was to some extent a paternal heritage. However, this French national identity was conditioned by three factors: First, the centralized, jacobine political and societal culture was certainly not part of the set of this convictions; a nation, which considered itself as "unique and indivisible", which denied any other identity, was incompatible for Schuman with his strong regional identity as a Lorrainer. Second, at the difference of most of his French compatriots, he married his French identity with deep understanding, even sympathy and respect for German culture and for Germany as such, for its cultural, political, economic and social dynamism, for his progressive system of social security, for the important role of Church and confessions in the public and even in the political sphere. That is the third reluctance Schuman had vis-à-vis France, and which marked his entire political life, especially during the inter-war era: The French laicism, the doctrine that the state was beyond all other things, beyond religion too, the claim that the state was entitled to expect more loyalty and higher authority than Church and faith – a conception Schuman could not share. In his eyes, subsidiarity was a fundamental principle for societal and political structures and powers – meaning that region and (civil) society should solve their problems autonomously as long as they were able to do so, without permanent submission to the centralized state. Schuman never declared himself a federalist, but his attitudes hint at a federal political and societal culture – more a German then than a French one. After all, he wanted to avoid at any rate to play the German version off against the French – this would always mean that Lorraine would be the victim.

It was these attitudes which led his fellow Lorrainers in Metz to push him to political responsibility, to defend the concerns and interests of Lorraine as well in the political arena. He himself still had no political ambitions; power as such did not have any appeal for him, and on the whole, personal modesty was and would always be the mark of his lifestyle, even when he became Prime Minister. He always preferred to travel with public transport, with train and bus, instead of an official car, sometimes at the dismal of his security service and bodyguards, who had to take care for him, and as Foreign Minister at the Quay d'Orsay he moved his office to a smaller, modest room instead of the opulent, spacious official ministerial office. Somewhat reluctantly, more by a feeling of duty than by predilection, he agreed to let himself be elected to the French Parliament, in 1919, and soon engages for the various special statutes Alsace and Lorraine had rescued from their German past into the French republic. That applies to bilingualism in those regions, but in particular for the Concordat with the Vatican, which granted a recognized role for the Churches in both regions, a status elsewhere unknown and unthinkable in secularist France, above all in the education system, one of the fields where the French state was particularly aggressive against all confessional schools. These conflicts came to an unprecedented height with the socialist government under Edouard Herriot, who was Prime Minister several times in the 20s and 30s and engaged in an exceptionally aggressive, atheistic anti-Church policy. Schuman acquired his reputation as a pugnacious deputy, who proved to be equally conciliant as tenacious.

After the outbreak of the Second World War and during the German "Blitzkrieg", Schuman is appointed Undersecretary of State for refugees – in the same government, where Charles de Gaulle assumed a role for the first time in his career. After the French surrender, Schuman moves, together with the legal (if not legitimate) French government under Marshall Pétain to Vichy but leaves as soon as he can to rejoin his home region

Lorraine, where the Nazis had put in place in the meantime Josef Bürckel as district leader, from the neighbouring German region Rhineland-Palatinate. Immediately after his arrival, Schuman is arrested and spends seven months in prison, before Bürckel sets him free, however under house arrest. Bürckel may have had the hope that Schuman was ready to collaborate with the German side – an entirely illusionary hope of course, which Schuman himself never nourished. On the contrary, in August 1942 he escapes from his gilded cage and spends the next years in several hideaways under wrong names in various monasteries, hosted by monks and abbots, who highly estimated his engagement for the Church.

Back to Metz after its liberation in 1944, the leading political circles receive him with reservation and mistrust – was he closer to the Nazis than he committed to be? Was he more loyal to the German cause than to the French, was he finally a "boche" (the swear word for Germans)? They declare him unelectable and eliminate him from political activity. Just General de Gaulle, who was himself sentenced to death by the General Pétain, head of the Vichy government, on the grounds of being a traitor, and who does now the same thing with General Pétain himself, just de Gaulle, the new strong leader, the statesman who united France again, lifts the ban over Schuman. De Gaulle has great esteem for his veracity and integrity, even if he was reported later on that he said about Schuman, when asked whether he was a reliable French patriot: "Schuman? A 'boche'. A good 'boche'. But a 'boche' anyway."[22]

---

22 „Schuman? Un Boche. Un bon Boche. Mais un Boche tout de même." This quotation from de Gaulle is mentioned in Jacques Binoche: Hitler, les Allemands et le Général de Gaulle. Paris 2015, Footnote 6. Margriet Krijtenburg: Schuman's Europe: his frame of reference. Leiden 2012, repeats the same remark of de Gaulle (p. 167) und Schuman's biographer does not omit the same quotation; see René Lejeune: Robert Schuman. Un Pére pour l'Europe. Metz 2013 (2nd edition), p. 127. De Gaulle was not the only one who called Schuman a „Boche": Raymond Poidevin mentions the exclamation of a communist deputy in the French National Assembly, who „welcomed" Schuman, reelected to Parliament after the war, with the similar words: „Injures encore lorsqu'en novembre 1947 le communiste Jaques Duclos accueille son arrivée à la Chambre des députés par un ‚Voilà le Boche' l'accusant d'être un ancien officier allemand et claironnant: ‚C'est un Boche, ce président du Conseil'. Profondément blessé, Robert Schuman n'oubliera jamais ces injures." Raymond Poidevin: Robert Schuman,

Robert Schuman is reelected deputy in the French National Assembly, now one of the most experienced deputies, he chairs the Financial Committee, becomes Finance Minister and even, in 1947-48, Prime Minister – in a precarious economic and social situation, when communists and gaullists alike threaten the political stability of France, in a political system, the Fourth Republic, burdened by permanent reshuffling of government and the weak position of the head of government – it happens rarely that a Prime Minister stays in office for more than ten months: During the twelve years long lifetime of the Fourth Republic, the officeholder changes 23 times ... When Robert Schuman becomes Foreign Minister, 26 July 1948, he holds this office for four and a half years – by far the best performance of any minister in the Fourth Republic. He still has to tackle with manyfold resistance, with largely divergent currents, with intrigue and malicious denigration aiming to undermine his personal reputation. His own readiness for conciliation, even reconciliation, for a European international order are interpreted as weakness or even treason. Communists and gaullists scorn and denigrate him as 'boche', his backing by the moderate socialists and conservative (Christian) democrats was halfhearted – France was far from taking a unanimous decision to lay the ground for a supranational community, be it only for coal and steel. It was the personal decision of a man at the margins of the French political spectrum, in contradiction to the majority of the political elite of the country. What was needed then was a particularly careful, tactical approach, even political ruse, if he wanted to succeed with this project. But this project was the peak, the highlight in Schuman's political life, his rendez-vous with history.

Still, one element is lacking: After all these considerations concerning Schuman's origins, his personality, his engagement it may seem plausible that he could adopt the ideas of Monnet. But there is an unexpressed assumption for him to master all the difficulties, a premise difficult to seize and hard to prove by means of unequivocal sources, for plausible reasons, however. What was at stake was to pardon a former enemy, even a "hereditary enemy" of France, to reach out to this enemy and recognize him

---

un itinéraire étonnant. Webpage oft he Robert Schuman Foundation, Paris; https://www.robert-schuman.eu/fr/robert-schuman-un-itineraire-etonnant.

as equal. Today it is (fortunately!) hard to understand what such a move meant at the time between French and Germans, between Europeans; one would have to dive deep into the deeply rooted traumata of enmity and recall them to their emotional surface, in order to measure the depth of the trench between the French and Germans was. To offer reconciliation to an enemy – that move postulates the existence of a set of values, which is hardly imaginable without a Christian canon of values, without Christian faith, at least in the case of Robert Schuman. To pardon an enemy and go for reconciliation, to consider such a move not as a shame, as dishonor, to replace retribution by reconciliation instead of considering retribution inevitably as justice, to concede equal dignity even to an enemy (and to one who had committed the worst crimes against humanity), to find a positive value in reconciliation – all this requires as a Christian faith and its fundamental set of values. And that was indeed the case of Robert Schuman, these convictions were a necessary (not sufficient) condition for him to stride over such deep crevasses as the immediate past had ripped. One will never find any notes or other official sources, which could lay open those underlying motives for Schuman – in the secularist French political culture they would have been meaningless and invalid arguments for political decision. And Schuman himself had never formulated such a commitment, which could serve as proof between his uncontestable Christian faith and his reconciling political action. These considerations stay therefore at the level of speculation, plausible speculation however, looking for the 'missing link', which enables us to fully understand Schuman's engagement for Monnet's plan.[23]

That were the preconditions for the first week of May 1950.

Schuman and Monnet – united in diversity

It is curious how close and at the same time how divergent the two personalities were, who found a common way to launch a revolutionary project

---

23 Alan Fimister comes close to confirm these hypotheses in his article: Integral Humanism and the Re-Unification of Europe. In: Sylvain Schirmann (Hrsg.): Robert Schuman et les Pères de l'Europe. Cultures politiques et années de formation. Actes du colloque de Metz du 10 au 12 octobre 2007, p. 25–38.

together in those early days of May 1950, a project that would pave the way for a supranational Europe, a Europe which would be conferred upon a share of national sovereignty. They were so different personalities: Whereas Robert Schuman was deeply rooted in his catholic convictions and committed publicly a large part of his political life to them, Jean Monnet war – at least publicly – indifferent with regard to religion; he never committed any religious faith, much less did he suggest that such a faith would be the premise and motive for his action. Whereas Schuman was lawyer, who in the last resort fought for justice and the rule of law, Jean Monnet was a businessman, entrepreneur, pragmatic. Whereas Schuman finally assumed political responsibility and made his way through the political institutions, Monnet stayed apart, never claimed to be elected, never assumed a political function. Whereas Schuman was obviously close to Germany, bilingual, with a double culture, Monnet was closer to the Anglo-Saxon world, to the United States and the United Kingdom, spoke fluently English. Whereas Schuman got engaged in intra-European, internal French, regional, at best bilateral (Franco-German) relations, Monnet was open to the world nearly from childhood on, Atlantic, in Northern Europe one would say: Hanseatic.

And still, the convergence between the two men are equally striking:

Both of them took some distance towards the mainstream of French national politics, towards the claim of the French nation state to define exclusively their identity, despite their undisputable loyalty to France. Both of them were skeptical vis-à-vis the French ideology of sovereignty and were thus free for more creative solutions in international relations. There political attitudes, their marginal position in the French jacobine Paris may even have been rooted in similar traditions: In the South-West that was the tradition of the "Girondistes", the anti-jacobine, anti-centralistic, federal heritage and its opposition against "Paris" – in the North-East it was the exceptional role and geopolitical position of Alsace and Lorraine, two regions, which always stood halfway between France and Germany, bilingual, bi-cultural, ever again victims of the conflict between the two nation states, always insisting on their autonomy, two regions, which never integrated entirely and without reserves into neither the one nor the other nation state and their claim of sovereignty. Both of them, Jean Monnet as much as Robert Schuman, were not a product of the Parisian elites, but looked at France from the margins.

Restart in May: "The Masterword is: Peace"[24]

Back to 1st of May in Paris, when Schuman was back from his private refuge close to Metz and declared that he was ready to adopt Monnet's plan and do his best to implement it. What that meant was further intense work on the text itself, on the other hand political tactical finesse, so that the expected opposition and resistance would not make the plan fail. And indeed, there was no doubt that there would be such opposition and resistance, refusal and maybe even outrage in the political arena and in public opinion. That opposition, expectedly, would as well come from the communist as from the Gaullist camp – from the communist, because they opposed any move not consecrated by Moscow, from the Gaullists, because they opposed any move, which would put national sovereignty at risk. Even if both political forces were not represented in the government, their influence on the political stance of France on the whole, not least via the National Assembly, was strong and Gaullist attitudes were even to be found with the Prime Minister, Georges Bidault, comme Bernard Clappier confirms: "One should not forget that Bidault's vision of the relations to Germany were close to those of the Gaullists."[25] "The obstacles were so high!", exclaims Schuman's biographer René Lejeune: "In Parliament, Gaullists and communists, supported by nationalists of all colors, would fiercely fight against any idea of a union with Germany, five years after the nightmare of the Nazi regime. And even more any steps abandoning national sovereignty. Within government, those forces hostile to any innovation of the kind would jeopardize any such project."[26]

Schuman, the next intimate in the small circle of "conspirators", as Jean Monnet called them, mobilized all his twenty years long political

---

24 Monnet, Mémoires, op.cit., p. 431.
25 „Il ne faut pas oublier qu'il y avait chez Bidault une vision proche de la vision gaulliste pour ce qui concerne les relations avec l'Allemagne." See Footnote 19.
26 Lejeune, Schuman, op.cit., p. 14.

experience to manoeuver the plan through the week without raising public attention.

In fact, the leading French newspaper Le Monde reported, 2nd May, on a meeting between Prime Minister Bidault and Jean Monnet, the meeting, Monnet had asked for, but which never had taken place![27] Another witness of the time and intimate of Schuman, one of the younger generation in Lorraine, Jean-Marie Pelt, relates[28] that Schuman had asked Bidault for a meeting to explain him the plan, suggesting a date he knew Bidault would be out of office, so that he, Schuman, would have the possibility to affirm that he had been willing to inform Bidault, but that it was him, Bidault, who was not available. At the same time Schuman, by this ruse, could avoid a probably unpleasant, if not awkward discussion.

However the details may have been, Wednesday, 3rd May, Schuman had to lay open, at least allusively, what he had in mind for next week's conference in London. The French government, as most of the governments of our nation states to until today, sat together in its weekly cabinet meeting, when Schuman announced in a few vague words[29] that he had a plan for the scheduled conference of the Foreign Ministers. Schuman must have handed over to Bidault, during or just after the meeting, a copy of the plan, since Bidault called Jean Monnet to report on the project the same afternoon, showing Monnet the copy with great indignation, accusing him: "Schuman showed me this paper, seems that is was you who wrote it. It would have appreciated to be informed first." Monnet retorted calmly that this had just been the case: "He looked for the letter, which he found

---

[27] Monnet, Mémoires, op.cit., p. 433: „Je n'eus pas le rendez-vous et cependant on pouvait lire dans Le Monde du mardi que j'avais été reçu par le président du Conseil!"

[28] So far Jean-Marie Pelt in the video produced by the Council of the European Union, „Europe through the Generations", https://www.youtube.com/watch?v=isVdxUBAp78). Pelt, one of the founding fathers of the French ecological movement, was well acquainted with Schuman and often invited to talk with him in his private house.

[29] In Jean Monnet's words: „en termes voilés", Mémoires, op.cit., p. 433; see Lejeune, Schuman, op.cit., p. 18, but he tells the story of this cabinet meeting with nearly the same words Monnet uses to sum up the meeting of 9th May – should he have mixed up the two meetings?

on his desk. Had he read it? In his memoirs he writes that this was the case and I believe him. No doubt that the plan did not comply with his own efforts to create a Transatlantic Council."[30]

Let us listen to Bidault himself: "The project had been transferred by Jean Monnet to the Hôtel Matignon [siege of the French government]. It has been reported that I did not understand its meaning. The truth is that I got the impression, the plan could be improved by some modifications or omissions, which would not have altered its structure. The permanent disturbances in times of unrest, the many strikes, the flurry of the trade unions, what was called the 'affaire of the generals', all this created an environment, which I did consider as not propitious for the corrections, which I considered as useful for the success of this far going initiative."[31] Jean Monnet, impatient as he was – continues Bidault – hurried up to rush over to the Foreign Minister and made the plan palatable for him.[32] A hardly trustable version of the story: Very important issues were

---

30 Monnet, Mémoires, op.cit., p. 434: „Il chercha la lettre, elle était sur son bureau. L'avait-il lue? Il assure que oui dans ses Mémoires, et je le crois. Sans doute ne répondait-elle pas à ses préoccupations du moment qui étaient de créer un Haut Conseil atlantique."

31 The original reads: „Le projet m'avait été porté à l'Hôtel Matignon par M. Jean Monnet. On a dit que je n'en avais pas compris l'intérêt. La vérité est que j'avais le sentiment que le plan pouvait être amélioré par certaines modifications ou suppressions qui n'auraient pas porté atteinte à sa structure. Le harcèlement d'une époque agitée, la multiplication des grèves, la nervosité syndicale et ce qu'on a appelé « l'affaire des généraux » constituaient un environnement peu favorable à l'établissement des quelques corrections que je jugeais utiles au succès de cette vaste entreprise. » Georges Bidault : D'une Résistance à l'autre. Paris: Les Presses du Siècle, 1965; online at CVCE : http://www.cvce.eu/obj/georges_bidault_d_une_resistance_a_l_autre_extrait_sur_le_plan_schuman-fr-fa58a5d0- 9d13-43b3-875d-592a6dbb57a1.html. The « affaires des généraux » was a scandal tiggered by the unauthorized publication of a report on the state of conditions in what was to become Vietman, i.e. in French « Indochina ». The author of the report was General Georges Revers, who was transferred for disciplinary reasons in 1949 and suspended in 1950.

32 In Bidaults moaning words: „Jean Monnet n'aime pas attendre quand il a une grande idée en tête. Il se précipita donc au Quai d'Orsay et y trouva un ministre avec lequel le commissaire au Plan avait eu maille à partir quand son interlocuteur était aux Finances. » Bidault, D'une Résistance á l'autre, op.cit., here quoted from CVCE, see Footnote 31.

at stake – the solution of the "German question"! –, the pressure of time was high, and Jean Monnet had by no means chosen the access to Schuman himself – chance, Clappier's accidental visit to Monnet's office, had opened the gateway to the Foreign Minister. Bernard Clappier has his own opinion concerning the silence of Bidault: His head of office, Pierre-Louis Gabriel Falaize, remembers Clappier, had thrown Monnet's draft in one of the deskdrawers in Bidault's office and therefore somewhat hidden away the dossier from the Prime Minister's eyes – whether on purpose or unintended is an open question. The most credible version is how Jean Monnet remembers himself the circumstances of the unfortunate communication with the Prime Minister.

In other words: Bidault alleges that he read the plan, but considered it as not mature, and explains the fact that he would have needed an additional delay of a couple of days to modify or adapt the plan by reference to the distraction imposed on him by political turbulences in internal French politics. By this version he suggests that he too would have implemented the plan, even if in a slightly different way than imagined by Monnet. This does not sound very convincing: Time was short, there were only ten days left before the deadline of the conference of the Foreign Ministers, where France was under pressure to deliver on the German question. And Bidault does not give any hint which modifications he would have wished for.

The question whether or not Bidault read the plan cannot be elucidate with certainty, but anyway – he implies it himself – did he have other, different conceptions of the future security politics of France. He was an "Atlanticist", put his hopes on a close cooperation with the United States, had just a week before, 16th April, in Lyon suggested the creation of a Transatlantic High Council, requiring a strong commitment of the United States to grant economic and external security to France. This maybe the real reason why Bidault was not interested in Monnet's Plan – and this is as well the assumption of Jean Monnet himself.

Finally, there are four explanations for the fact that Bidault did not make the plan his own affair: First, it may well be that he just did not take notice of Monnets communication that Friday, 28th April, and unintendedly shifted the initiative to Schuman, leaving to him the intellectual and political property, so to say. Second, Bidault leaned more on the side of the Gaullist camp, as Clappier states, and therefore was skeptical if not hostile against any transfer for sovereignty and any supranational Franco-German Union. Third, he pursued his own agenda aiming at stabilizing Europe's post-war order, emphasizing the project of institutionalizing the Transatlantic relations. However, the probability of such an evolution had already faded away in early May 1950. And, fourth, he may simply not have seized the importance and potential scope of Monnet's plan or at least underestimated them.[33] These four explanations are not necessarily mutually exclusive – Bidault's disinterest in Monnet's plan, at a first glance he may have had on the paper, may have induced him, because of his skepticism with regard to any transfer of sovereignty, to work on his own ideas … but this is speculation, which will never find a proof.

After all, one might advance two conjectures, which are highly probable: The fact that Bidault summoned Monnet only Wednesday, after the cabinet meeting, after Schuman had (evasively) talked about the plan and had given him a copy, and that he, Bidault, was still emotionally upset at that moment, suggests that he had not read the plan before; otherwise he had had the opportunity to hold Monnet accountable for his proceedings. And, second: It is for sure that the plan would have had an altogether different future, had Bidault read it, and not left unintendedly the initiative to Schuman, it would have been narrowed down or directed towards entirely different aims, but it would have anyway lost its revolutionary impetus: the overcoming of national sovereignty in favour of supranational European integration, equality with Germany in a partnership with the Federal Republic. In other words, and that makes this detailed investigation relevant: If the French Prime Minister, Georges Bidault, had taken the time, between Friday, 28th April, and Wednesday, 3rd May (i.e. before the cabinet meeting that day), to read and think about Monnet's dossier,

---

33 „Certains ont pensé que le plan Schuman aurait pu être un plan Bidault si ce dernier avait eu connaissance du document, mais je ne le crois pas. Je ne crois pas qu'il y ait eu un 'rendez-vous manqué de Bidault avec l'Histoire', comme il a été écrit. Bidault a donné son accord lorsqu'il a été mis au courant, mais je pense que c'est parce qu'il n'a pas compris tout de suite la portée de la proposition, ce qu'elle impliquait pour l'avenir. Il ne faut pas oublier qu'il y avait chez Bidault une vision proche de la vision gaulliste pour ce qui concerne les relations avec l'Allemagne." Clappier, L'Europe une longue marche, op.cit., p. 25.

which he had received that Friday, then the European Community would not have come into existence, or at least not in the way that it did.[34] This is a statement of such a fundamental kind that we will come back to it in the second part of this book, when the narrative has been given and the time has come to think about it.

Obviously, Bidault let go things as they went, presumably slightly disapproving, but reluctantly tolerating them, and, due to the flat hierarchy in the government of the Fourth Republic, without really having the institutional standing to interfere with an initiative of the Foreign Minister. The cabinet on the whole did not raise any objection, however probably because of a nearly complete ignorance of the content and meaning of the plan, if Schuman was really so evasive and vague about this initiative, telling his colleagues that it was about coal and steel (not about sovereignty), a balancing of interests (not reconciliation) between France and Germany, something the Western allies required (not an entirely new approach) ... Anyway, Schuman, Monnet and their intimates could continue to work on the plan after 3rd May; they had circumnavigated the cliff of the inevitable information of the Prime Minister and the cabinet.

And indeed, the eighth, they formulated the second last version of the plan the following day, 4th May. As Jean Monnet noted on the text of the previous variant, the one of 28th April, it was now, 4th May, that he sent the text to René Mayer, Minister of Justice, another old friend since the first months of the Second World War, when Jean Monnet was in London, charged by the French government with the mission to negotiate an integration, a fusion of both the British and the French armies in the (forthcoming) battle against Germany – very similar to his tasks in the First World War. Mayer committed himself "immediately and enthusiastically to the plan, where he found an echo of our talks in Algiers, when we were

---

34 Jean Monnet himself was not very much in favour of such counterfactual speculations: „Ce que fût devenu le projet entre ses mains, et l'Europe au bout du compte, d'autres se sont posé la question. Pour moi, je ne me suis jamais demandé de ma vie quelles conséquences aurait pu avoir une situation qui ne s'est pas produite. C'est l'exercice le plus stérile qui soit. Le fait est qu'il n'y a pas eu de plan Bidault, mais un plan Schuman." Monnet, Mémoires, op.cit., p. 434.

discussed the necessity to rebuild Europe in peace."[35] René Mayer was now himself member of the French government, as much as René Pleven, another member of Monnet's former delegation to London and now minister for the French overseas territories, a couple of weeks later minister of defense and for some time even Prime Minister. Both of them should and would, as intimate friends of Monnet, play a decisive role in pushing the plan through at governmental level (and even extend their role later in 1950, when Pleven proposed a European Defense Community, very much along the line of the Coal and Steel Community).

Saturday, 6th May, the ninth version of the plan was finalized and Monnet decided that this should be indeed the final one. Equipped with this version, Monnet, accompanied by René Mayer, rendered himself to the office of Robert Schuman. Once more, modifications had been made mainly in order to meet the diplomatic considerations a Foreign Minister had to respect: "France, championing since more than twenty years a united Europe, always aimed at serving the cause of peace. Europe has not been created, we plunged into the war."[36] – "That was a reminder of Briand, but at the same time a rejection to any rhetoric", explains Jean Monnet himself this new initial sentence; and what follows was, according to him, a commitment to "the fundamental decision to adopt a method aiming at integration ever more the factual reality and the mentalities."[37]: "Europe will not be made all at once, or according to a single plan. It will be built through concrete achievements which first create a de facto solidarity." But then the ever renewed overhauling of the text should definitely end: "'Now we have to come to an end', I said, and wrote on the text: 'definitive, Saturday, 3 p.m.'"

And still – one additional idea slipped into this ninth version, at the demand of René Mayer; the ninth version, despite what Monnet noted, is therefore not the last, not the last one. To be precise, the version Robert Schuman read to the public three days later, the real "Schuman Plan", is

---

35 Ibidem, p. 435.
36 Schuman Declaration, here quoted from the EU webpage: https://european-union.europa.eu/principles-countries-history/history-eu/1945-59/schuman-declaration-may-1950_en
37 Monnet: Mémoires, op.cit., p. 434.

in fact the tenth version. Only here and then this sentence occurs: "With increased resources Europe will be able to pursue the achievement of one of its essential tasks, namely, the development of the African continent."[38] This sentence must have been added soon after the final formulation of the ninth version, since Monnet "immediately sent the documents to Pleven [...] Thus ended the list of addressees. On the whole, eleven people were initiated to the secret."[39]

Let us make sure who these eleven people were: First of all, Jean Monnet himself, of course, the inventor of the whole plan and who knew therefore its baseline first. Monnet had informed Bernard Clappier, orally, 13th or 14th April, at the eve of the first talk Monnet had with Paul Reuter, 14th April, a talk deepened the next day, 15th April. Sunday, 16th April, at home in Houjarray, Monnet called in Etienne Hirsch, together they elaborated the first written version of the plan, which Monnet's secretary, Suzanne Miguez, typewrote Monday, 17th April (Madame Miguez, who typewrote all the successive versions too must have been one of the best acquainted people with the text ...). Hirsch, under the cover of confidentiality, asked two representative personalities of the concerned French industrial associations, Roger Cadel and Alexis Aron, how the plan would be perceived in the French coal and steel industries. Monday, 17th April, Pierre Uri joined the group, and then for ten days nothing serious happened, until the decisive moment of 28th April, when Monnet tried in vain to get the plan through to Prime Minister Georges Bidault, via Pierre-Louis Falaize, his head of office – both of them did not take notice and must therefore not be counted among the initiates. On the other hand, Robert Schuman did spend time with the plan, during the weekend of 29th and 30th April, to think Jean Monnet's proposals through and agreed, declaring that he would walk the line on Monday, 1st May. Two days later, 3rd May, at the occasion of the weekly cabinet meeting, Schuman officially informed Bidault, who got to read the text now, but Schuman's communication with the cabinet was apparently so superficial that it cannot be considered as informed or acquainted. 4th of May, René Mayer was drawn

---

38 Schuman Declaration, see Footnote 36.
39 Monnet: Mémoires, op.cit., p. 435.

Restart in May: "The Masterword is: Peace"[24] 45

into the group of intimates, as well as, two days later, René Pleven – at the Moment when the plan was, in its ninth version, and more precisely even only in its tenth version, mature, definite. "Nine persons were informed", writes Monnet, but leaving aside the two representatives of the industry, and it is indeed not for sure what they precisely got to know – probably not a written copy of the then topical version. Anyway, Suzanne Miguez was number twelve, and even Falaize, number thirteen, had probably been informed by Bidault, in the meantime.

Two (or three?) more got to know the plan over the weekend: Sunday morning, Monnet went to the office of Robert Schuman, where he met him together with Bernard Clappier. In the meantime, they had informed the General secretary of the Foreign Ministry, Alexandre Parodi, about the plan – a delicate move, not without a hidden agenda: The Minister could officially declare later on that "the Ministry" had been informed and that he had therefore complied with the professional standards of the institution. But at the same time, Schuman had imposed an Parodi strict confidentiality, i.e. despite his function as head of the whole diplomatic and administrative stuff of the Ministry, he was denied to pass over any information to any member of the stuff. "We were firmly determined", writes Monnet, "to conduct the whole operation apart from the diplomatic channels and renounce any ambassador."[40] What they feared was obviously the opposition of the whole diplomatic corps against any encroachment on the French national sovereignty – if anywhere, it was here that the hard core of the defense of national sovereignty was to be found, all the more so since such a move would inevitably lead to sharing power in external relations, and that means a loss of power for the concerned people themselves. The Foreign Minister had to circumvent his own stuff, considered with mistrust and lack of loyalty in the case, in order to prevent his plan from failing.

Another person got to know the plan over the weekend, somewhat unexpectedly, but very usefully, as things worked out over the following week: The American Foreign Minister. Dean Acheson stayed in Paris as an interstation on his way to the conference in London, which would last

---

40 Ibidem.

from Wednesday to Saturday. The rhythm of such conferences were still different from what it is today, slower, unhurried, with more time to think better of the upcoming issues – a whole week for such a meeting?! Unthinkable today! But at the time, a slowed-down, or better: a not yet accelerated diplomatic agenda of this kind was still the ordinary one. Anyway, Acheson, accompanied by the American ambassador in Paris, David Bruce, not only met of course with his French colleague – what is more: they knew each other very well and estimated each other. Jean Monnet too was a personal friend of Acheson's, his multiple and prolonged stays in Washington during the World War had brought him in contact with Acheson, in various functions, but private as well and with a personal friendship in their wake. And as Monnet was anyway well acquainted, doing business with American commercial partners on behalf of his Cognac producing family, with the American way of reaching deals; he knew the criteria and mechanisms of Acheson's discernment.

Schuman and Monnet could not do anything else than initiate Acheson to the plan – any other proceeding would have been considered by Acheson as a betrayal of trust, next Wednesday: 'Three days before we sat together for a confidential meeting', Acheson would have said to Schuman (or at least he would have thought it), 'and you did not inform me about your revolutionary plan?!' There was no alternative, Acheson had to be made an intimate, and that was not entirely without risk. Indeed, at a first glance, Acheson was had some doubts, very American doubts: Wasn't this a sort of European planned, command economy for coal and steel, politically directed – instead of liberal and market based? For an American, this was a horrible perspective, all the more so since the block antagonism between the two superpowers was just about this all-decisive issue: the freedom of the market or state directed planned economy. At this moment, it proved to be particularly useful that Monnet immediately seized the problem of perception, that he knew how to help Acheson out of his doubt, how to sell the plan to an American – by insisting on the fact that it was all about a large, transborder, transnational market just without state driven intervention, and not at all a planned economy, that political intervention was at best needed to grant the functioning of the large market, but not to impose modes of production and consumption, to grant competition, but not to support the privileges of cartels etc. Acheson was convinced and that in turn proved to be very important next Wednesday in London, when the acceptance of the French plan was at stake among the Western Allies – something far from being accomplished in advance, taking into account the outrage and fierce resistance of the British Foreign Minister Ernes Bevin; more about this dispute later ... That Sunday 7th May anyway, the list of the initiates was now definitely closed; it comprised, in addition to the eleven, or thirteen (with Madame Miguez and Falaize), now sixteen on the whole: Numbers 14, 15 and 16 were Alexandre Parodi, Dean Acheson and David Bruce.

But that was of course not enough to lay the plan open to the public and travel to London ...

III Europe Day

From Paris to Bonn: Mischlich's "Mission impossible"

Obviously, Schuman needed two more things: One was the official agreement of the French government. Without such a formal adoption of the project he would not have been entitled to speak on behalf of France next Wednesday in London. And, equally important, Schuman had to make sure that the (West-)Germans would go along with his plan – if he proposed his initiative in the French government and the in London, but the Germans would afterwards rebuff it, then a diplomatic catastrophe would be the inevitable outcome and consequence, the solution of the German problem as it was in line with French interests would prove to be unreachable, Schuman's position untenable. The cabinet meeting of the upcoming week had been advanced, by the initiated ministers, under pretext, from Wednesday to Tuesday, 9th May – Wednesday Schuman would have to show up in London[41] – so that the plan could be officially endorsed by the government. Until this decisive moment, the German agreement had to be reached. Sunday, 7th May, the initiated actors knew what they had to do until Tuesday evening: obtain the German agreement and make the French government adopt the plan as the official stance of France.

But both things were easier to conceive than to realize: *How* could the agreement of Germans be acquired over one day and a half? The normal procedure would have been to inform the French office holder – not yet an ambassador, but a "High Commissioner", since West-Germany was still under occupation regime – in the Federal Republic, François Poncet, and to mandate him with the mission to ask for a meeting with the German chancellor, arguing for his agreement with the French plan. The chancellors, because Schuman had no direct German counterpart, just because of the occupation statute, which the Allies maintained even after the foundation of the Federal Republic, which then was not allowed to rebuild

---

[41] Monnet, Mémoires, op.cit., p. 436: „Pleven et Mayer firent en sorte que le conseil se tint exceptionnellement le mardi matin. Le secret devait être total jusque-là."

a Foreign Office, neither have a Foreign Minister; the Allies denied any autonomous, left alone sovereign foreign policy to the new West German state. The chancellor himself had to assume the tasks which inevitably occurred between the Federal Republic and other countries, and Konrad Adenauer took this responsibility very seriously, so much so that he only very reluctantly conferred it to another minister when the Foreign Office was finally allowed to emerge again as the agency for West-Germany's external relations, from the middle of the 50s on. But Schuman did not want to go the way via official diplomacy anyway, because he did not even trust in his own diplomatic stuff, his own ministry, convinced that they were not ready to overcome the inherited spell and burden of national sovereignty. Theoretically there was the option for Schuman to travel to Bonn in person – but neither was there enough time for such a move nor would it be possible without attracting all the attentiveness of those who should not be drawn into the secret procedure.

There was only one option left: "The personal contact Schuman wanted to establish with Adenauer, would be conferred upon somebody of his own office, someone who would be sent do Bonn secretly, exactly at the same hour, when the decision had to be taken. This hour had still to be fixed"[42] ... and how this intimate could be: Schuman's choice was another young Lorrainer, the German speaking Robert Mischlich, who for a couple of years already went back and forth between the Ministry of Justice and the Ministry of Foreign Affairs, because he was entrusted in the Ministry of Justice with the cautious adaptation or maintenance of specific

---

42 Monnet, Mémoires, a.a.O., S. 435: „Notamment, le contact personnel que Schuman désirait prendre avec Adenauer serait confié à un membre de son cabinet qui irait secrètement à Bonne à l'heure même de la décision. Restait à fixer cette heure." See there considerations on the exact moment. Monnet's account is not entirely correct this time: The young man Schuman had called to his office, Robert Mischlich, was not member of Schuman's team, but civil servant in the Ministry of justice; see the follow-up of the story. See again as well the interview with Clappier, quoted several times. Mischlich himself comments on the conjecture that Adenauer had been informed in advance: „Tout cela est inexact. Le témoignage de Bernard Clappier est à cet égard capital et irréfutable."; Robert Mischlich: Une mission secrète à Bonn. Lausanne 1986, Jean Monnet Foundation, p. 56.

legal rules in Alsace and Lorraine, a terrain particularly precious for Schuman, as we know. An intimate for Schuman, with the same attachment to their common home region, with very similar concerns in the French national governance system which had occupied Schuman himself for so long a time (and still did), and with the additional advantage that he was not a diplomat, which relieved Schuman from his duty to justify his choice of this young and largely unexperienced man within the hierarchy of his own ministry. And Mischlich had already accompanied Schuman to Bonn twice before, in August 1949 and in January 1950 – he was thus well acquainted with the problems of Franco-German relations and did not need an extra initiation and preparation.

"Early in the morning of 8th May", writes Mischlich himself, "Robert Schuman called me to his office. I went immediately to his modest office, which he had prepared for himself at Quai d'Orsay. There, and not in the gorgeous Bureau de Vergennes [the official ministerial office], he normally did his work, studied dossiers and received close collaborators. The minister told me without delay, that he would entrust me with a tricky and secret mission."[43] Mischlich is indeed the only one who could give an account of this mission – just because it was top secret; except Schuman, only Monnet and Clappier knew about it. That is the reason why the Jean Monnet Foundation in Lausanne invited Mischlich much later, in 1986, to lay down the memories of the only episode in his life of public interest – the only authentic report of the only actor involved in this mission between the morning of 8th and the late morning of 9th May, of not much more than 24 hours, which became decisive for the start of European integration.

This is why we follow now the traces of Mischlich and list to him, when he tells the story of these hours. "As time was short, Schuman told me: 'You will render yourself to Bonn this evening and meet with Chancellor Adenauer tomorrow before noon. You will hand over to him personally two letters, one of which is the summary of the plan I shall submit to the [French] cabinet tomorrow, 9th May.' My mission was then entirely clear and precise and timed with rare accuracy. The minister added: 'There

---

43 See previous footnote.

are only very few people – among them Jean Monnet and Bernard Clappier of course – who know about the mission I am must conferring on you and which must be kept secret until its successful end. I very much insist on this aspect because the slightest indiscretion could make a project fail which I consider as of highest importance.' He then added as well [...] 'Chancellor Adenauer is not initiated, for nothing of what has been prepared Rue de Martignac [Jean Monnet's office] has been communicated to Bonn or proposed there.'" Mischlich was deeply impressed by this mission of course and continues: "Meet a German chancellor at a certain moment without any preparatory contact, and all this without any backing by the French diplomacy and by François Poncet himself – that seemed to me a particularly difficult task and did not hide my doubts away from Schuman. With some malicious humor he opposed: 'This task is not beyond your skills. Anyway, in some moments of life, providence [la grâce d'état] is on your side.' I took my leave, and he did not even wish good luck. The same evening, I took the train to Bonn."[44] Jean Monnet confirms the exact moment of Mischlich's leave: "In the evening, Clappier confirmed that the Schuman's collaborator, a lawyer from Lorraine, Michlich [sic¡] had left for Bonn."[45]

Mischlich took the night train from Paris to Bonn. He must have spent a nervous night in that train – burdened with this mission! A young man, largely unknown to those he was supposed to meet – Adenauer, in his memoirs, talks about "a French mister, whose name I do not know"[46] – and now advised by the French Foreign Minister himself, to hand over the two envelopes in his briefcase personally and exclusively to the German chancellor, to renounce any support by the French 'Ambassador', and even to strictly avoid that he became to know his presence in Bonn! How should this young man make his way into the Chancellor's office?! And, supposed he really got into the building, how would he find his way to the Chancellor himself?

---

44 Mischlich, Mission secrète, op.cit., p. 58.
45 Monnet, Mémoires, op.cit., p. 437.
46 Konrad Adenauer: Erinnerungen 1945–1963. Stuttgart 1964, p. 331.

9th May, around 9 a.m., Mischlich arrived at the Palais Schaumburg, then the siege of the Chancellor. "Two guards in uniform, who seemed to be embalmed for eternity, stood in front of the small palace as if it was a branch of Walhalla, siege of the German heroes after their death. With a grim face, I confronted them directly and cried in their faces my name, with the 'doctor' title, a title, which still has a magical effect in Germany today. I was not wrong: The two guards saluted and I still hear the sound of their boots in my ears today, when the clacked their heels together, at the same moment when I crossed the threshold of the Chancellor's office." What would be certainly impossible today, Mischlich achieved it: He had made it into the Chancellor's office.

In the building, he directed himself to the office of Herbert Blankenhorn, the closest advisor in foreign affairs to the Chancellor. Himself diplomat of career since the early 30s, he stayed in the Foreign Office during the Nazi period, as chief of protocol, in the last stage of his career. But Adenauer had not much choice – if he did not want to rely on entirely unexperienced amateur diplomates, he could only come back to those who had made their experiences with the Nazis; the problem has been discussed and disputed many times in post-war German historiography and public, and Blankenhorn himself was uncontroversial in this context.[47] Obviously, Mischlich had succeeded to remind him at least that he had accompanied Schuman in January to Bonn. "I implored him to do his very best to make me meet the Chancellor as soon as possible. He embraced my request immediately and went away with the two envelopes, which I had to deliver, to see the Chancellor himself. He even interrupted a cabinet meeting, where the German membership in the Council of Europe was at stake and took notice as well of the French proposal as of Schuman's personal letter. He discussed the issue at length with Blankenhorn, until Blankenhorn finally came back to me and informed me that the Chancellor was now ready to receive me." Mischlich succeeded even with this request! He made it into

---

[47] See Birgit Ramscheid: Herbert Blankenhorn (1904–1991). Adenauers außenpolitischer Berater. Düsseldorf 2006, in particular p. 135, in the chapter „Außenpolitische Anfänge 1949/50".

the Chancellor's office, to the Chancellor himself, and managed the get the two envelopes in his own hands!

Now there was only one thing lacking: Adenauer's agreement, which Mischlich had to report without any delay to Paris, because the French government met there just at the same time. Robert Schuman, assisted by Bernard Clappier, longed for the 'green light' from Bonn, with growing inquietude. Only then could Schuman inform the French cabinet a bit more in detail and ask his colleagues to mandate him to propose the plan on behalf of France to the two other allies, the next day in London, as the French solution to the German problem. All depended on hours, half hours, quarters of an hour, that morning. "It was around 11 a.m., when I entered the office of the Chancellor", writes Mischlich – only one hour before the deadline Schuman had set and which had to be respected by any means, because the French cabinet meeting was scheduled to come to an end around noon. I Schuman had not have the opportunity to take the floor and obtain the endorsement of the government – the plan would not have been proposed to the two other Western allies, the first European Community would not have come into existence, at least not at that moment of history. One hour to go ...

Konrad Adenauer, the European from Cologne

But who was the man in fact Mischlich met in the Palais Schaumburg? Who was Konrad Adenauer – this first Chanceloor of the Federal Republic, record holder for half a century, as far as the duration of this mandate is concerned, a new German myth, and not only for that reason? Adenauer was one decade older than Robert Schuman, born in 1876, deeply rooted in his home city, Cologne – son of a secretary at the court of appeal in Cologne, a pupil at the catholic school of Sankt Aposteln, third of five children. Just as Schuman, Adenauer choses a lawyer's career, leaves Cologne only shortly to study elsewhere, comes back to the Rhineland as soon as possible, first to Bonn, then to Cologne, where he successfully finished his studies. Soon after the turn of the century, he is employed by various courts, then works for local politicians and the assumes political responsibility himself. Several blows of fate burden his personal life: Twelve years after their marriage, in 1916, his first wife dies, leaving three children. He himself is seriously hurt in a car accident, the following year, and has to be operated in face and jaw. In 1919 he gets married for the second time and gives birth to another five children.

Notwithstanding all these obstacles, he becomes mayor of Cologne in 1927, at the young age of 41, a function, which corresponds perfectly to his ambitions and which he even assumes again for a short time after the Second World War. Between 1921 and the beginning of the Nazi period in 1933 he is one of the most high-ranking politicians of the Republic of Weimar, the first German democracy, after the end of the Monarchy. Adenauer is elected and several times reelected President of the Prussian Council – the Parliamentary chamber, which represents at the level of Prussian state – itself member state of the German Reich – the interests of the provinces, and these, especially those of the Rhineland, are indeed a primary concern for Adenauer: He does his best to dampen the centralizing rigor of the Prussian government. With the stronghold of his home town Cologne and the function of President of Parliament, Adenauer is for more than a decade an essential political figure in the German republic (of Weimar) – until the Nazis throw him out of office at all levels, as early as 13th March 1933.

> "When the newly appointed Chancellor of the Reich, Adolf Hitler, traveled to Cologne, 17th February 1933, for a big electoral campaign event, Adenauer did not receive him personally at the airport and denied an illumination of the Rhine to his honor. Adenauer argued that Hitler comes as leader of the party, not as Chancellor. Moreover, Adenauer asked for Swastika-flags to be eliminated from the bridge over the Rhine, on the grounds that they had been fixed on public property."

That was the irrevocable rupture with the Nazis, who identified Adenauer now as their enemy. "The week between national and local elections [the last one took place 12th March 1933] was for Adenauer a smear campaign when he got multiple warnings and threats. In front of the city-hall they cried "Adenauer away" and "shoot down Adenauer". For his pretended 'security', SA-guards were sent to his home. At the same time, other SA-members walked through the city and collected money under the slogan 'every shilling a shot against Adenauer!' [...] Leading drivers of this agitation were the Nazi newspapers 'Westdeutscher Beobachter' and the Rhenish Nazi-official Josef Grohé, who called Adenauer a 'slave of the Jews', 'bloody Jew' and 'Jewish swank of Cologne'. These malicious allegations hinted to Adenauer's good relations with Jews as e.g. the entrepreneur Dannie Heinemann and to the Jewish community as well as to the Zionist movement in Cologne."[48] The following year he is arrested for the first time by the Gestapo, the Nazi secret policy, and will be bullied ever again until the end of the war, with several stays in prison, the last time in 1944. This had of course consequences on his private life too: "After being arrested 23rd August, after escaping from the Gestapo-Prison on the exhibition grounds of Cologne and hiding close the small city of Hachenburg, Westerwald, his second wife, Gussie Adenauer, was harassed by the Nazis in the Gestapo headquarters in Cologne to the extent that she revealed where her husband had hidden himself. Consequently, Adenauer was arrested again 25th September 1944, the day of their silver wedding. She suffered from a psychological breakdown and tried to commit suicide. She never recovered from the sufferings of that time. She died 3rd March 1948 from the aftereffect of her injuries."[49]

Immediately after the liberation of the entirely destroyed city of Cologne by American troops, Adenauer was appointed Mayor again by their commanders – a rehabilitation, which did not last long, since soon after the British had replaced the Americans, Adenauer fell from grace with the new masters. "Trigger of this new dismissal by the British Brigadier Barraclough was a dispute over the ban prohibiting fuel [for heating houses] for the population. They accused him of 'incapacity' and 'lack of energy'. Probably his contacts to representatives of the French military administration played a role as well, because he was denied all sort of political activity and any access to the city of Cologne."[50] He was quickly rehabilitated though, but this further humiliation must have deeply shocked him.

---

48 Konrad Adenauer Stiftung: Absetzung Konrad Adenauers als Kölner Oberbürgermeister durch die Nationalsozialisten; https://www.kas.de/web/geschichte-der-cdu/kalender/kalender-detail/-/content/absetzung-konrad-adenauers-als-koelner-oberbuergermeister-durch-die-nationalsozialisten.
49 Konrad Adenauer Stiftung: Konrad Adenauer - Adenauer, Auguste („Gussie") Amalie Julie geb. Zinsser; https://www.konrad-adenauer.de/wegbegleiter/a/adenauer-gussie.
50 Konrad Adenauer Stiftung: Konrad Adenauer; https://www.konrad-adenauer.de/biographie/politischer-wiederaufstieg-1945-1949.

Despite all these obstacles, Adenauer, now close to 70, embraced his destiny and started to engage not only on the local, but soon again the level of the newly emerging West-German state, the Federal Republic. He took a leading role in the foundation of the Christian-Democratic Party, was elected its president and, after their electoral victory at the first general elections after the foundation of the Federal Republic 15th September 1949, Chancellor – not even eight months before Schuman reached out to him with his plan. Adenauer started immediately after taking office his own first attempts to launch European cooperation, and the British officer who dismissed him in 1945 was probably right in assuming that Adenauer aimed in particular at reconciliation with France – in his eyes, this was the silver bullet to prevent all future conflict and disaster, and the straight way towards European pacification and unification. Only a couple of weeks before 9th May 1950, early this same year, he had proposed himself a comprehensive integration of the West-German and the French economy – but Germany, the Federal Republic, had not yet the moral standing, five years after the war, to assume the role of a trustable initiator of such plans, and Adenauer's project had, at the difference of Jean Monnet's, the inconvenient to ask too much in terms of surrender of national, and after all French sovereignty – Germany had not much so surrender ... Adenauer's proposal was left without response and effect.

In those days around 9th May, German European politics was central to the German governmental preoccupations, for other reasons: What was at stake, was whether the Federal Republic should follow the invitation to join the Council of Europe, founded 5th May 1949, at a moment, when the new West-German state did not yet exist. The Council of Europe was initially meant to become the "engine" for European (federal) integration, but it soon became evident that it did and would not meet the expectations. The Council lacked any competence for binding legislation, for "supranational" decision-making, and it was in particular the United Kingdom, which blocked any advance in this direction. Still, the Council of Europe, in early 1950, spread hope and Adenauer advocated wholeheartedly German membership. In April he gave a speech in Parliament where he argued: "It is a question of existential destiny whether the German people wants Europe to be split between the great power-blocks of the United States and the Soviet Union, split into nation states, which will ever struggle with each other politically and oppose each other economically, or whether Europe achieves an economic and political unification, which allows for an emerging own political weight and internal stability. The Council of Europe, despite its weaknesses, is the until now the only way to achieve these goals."[51]

And now there was Robert Mischlich, sent by Robert Schuman, proposing another option …

"The James Bond of the French Diplomacy"[52]
Robert Mischlich and his tête-à-tête with Adenauer
(Palais Schaumburg, Bonn)

Just after the last quotation from Adenauer's Memoirs, he opens the chapter entitled "The Schuman Plan". It starts with an account of the cabinet meeting, that same morning 9th May, in Bonn as in Paris, and was dedicated to the question of the Federal Republic's joining of the Council of Europe. "The cabinet meeting started at 9.30h. It was very important that the government took a decision. A conference of the three Western Minister of Foreign affairs was scheduled to take place 11th [sic!] in London, which would focus on the German question. It was absolutely necessary that the German government took a decision, before this conference started, concerning its readiness to cooperate within the Council of Europe. I was convinced of the outstanding importance of this decision, taken 9th May in the cabinet, and had therefore conveyed a press conference that same evening at 8 p.m., in order to inform the German and foreign public alike and at the same time about this decision." Then follows

---

51 Adenauer, Erinnerungen, op.cit., p. 330.
52 So Mischlich himself, ironical and in a humorous sense for sure, in a letter to Paul Collowald, who had urged him to write down his memories of his travel to Bonn: „Vielleicht haben Sie ja den Eindruck, dass ich während dieser 48 Stunden der James Bond der französischen Diplomatie war, aber die Dinge lagen in Wirklichkeit viel einfacher." See Paul Collowald: Die Kontroverse, siehe footnote 64, p. 90.

the important sentence: "In the morning, I did not yet know that this day would become a turning point in the European development."[53]

Since so much depends now on days, and indeed on hours, we must first question Adenauer's irritating indication that the conference of the Foreign Ministers was scheduled 11th May – this is formally correct, but formally only, because in reality it began already 10th May, with the decision on the Schuman plan, and continued indeed over the next three days, until 13th May. There is some good reason to suppose that Adenauer was mistaken concerning the date: Otherwise it would be hard to understand why the German cabinet meeting, as much as the French one, had been advanced to Tuesday, 9th May, instead of its normal meeting day, which was Wednesday. The same argument is valid for Adenauer's intention to hold a press conference that same evening – equally as in Paris! – in order to explain the German position publicly just before the conference of the Foreign Ministers started.

> "During the deliberation in the cabinet, I got the information that a special envoy of the French Foreign Minister Schuman wanted to communicate an important message to me personally. Assistant Secretary of State Blankenhorn received the man, who handed over to him two letters of Schuman. The content of these letters would be extremely urgent, he said, they had to be submitted to me immediately. The French envoy, whose name I do not know, informed Blankenhorn that the French cabinet was meeting at the same hour in Paris and was deliberating the content of these letters. Foreign Minister Schuman would be very grateful if he

---

53 Adenauer, Erinnerungen, op.cit., p. 331. See as well his gratefulness vis-à-vis Schuman when the Elysée-Treaty was signed! During the negotiations over this treaty, often erroneously understood as the beginning of Franco-German "Friendship", Adenauer wrote to Schuman, 10th September 1962: „Lieber Herr Schumann [sic!] – Während des Besuchs des General de Gaulle in der vergangenen Woche habe ich oft Ihrer gedacht als des Mannes, der durch den Vorschlag der Montanunion den Grundstein legte zu der Freundschaft, die nunmehr unsere beiden Länder so eng miteinander verbindet. – Unserer gemeinsamen Arbeit gedenke ich immer in Dankbarkeit. Es drängt mich gerade bei diesem Anlaß meiner Dankbarkeit Ihnen gegenüber Ausdruck zu geben. – Es wäre mir eine sehr große Freude, wenn wir uns noch einmal wiedersehen würden. – Mit sehr herzlichen Grüßen, Ihr Konrad Adenauer". Facsimile of the hand-written letter in Marie-Thérèse Bitsch: Robert Schuman. Apôtre de l'Europe. 1953-1963. Brussels, 2010, p. 334.

could immediately be informed about my opinion on these letters. Blankenhorn handed both letters over to me in the cabinet room."

Adenauer, statesman as he was, seized immediately the importance of the proposal, and Schuman's personal letter left no doubt that he was right: "The essence of Robert Schuman's proposal was, to submit the entire French and German coal, steel and iron industry [...] under a common High Authority". Such a move would "create the first firm foundation of a European Federation, indispensable for the maintenance of peace in Europe. – In his personal letter to me, Schuman wrote that the purpose of his proposal was not economic, but eminently political", in so far as it was meant to secure peace between the two countries.[54] Adenauer did not hesitate a second: "Schuman's plan complied entirely with my own ideas, which I had put forward many times", and in the evening, when he explained the plan in the press conference to a large public, he underlined in ever renewed effort the outstanding importance and meaning of the plan, after explaining the government's decision to join the Council of Europe: "I insist firmly that I consider it [Schuman's plan] as a magnanimous move of France and his Foreign Minister Schuman towards Germany and European question. It is without any doubt of the greatest importance for the relations between France and German and for the whole of the European evolution. [...] I consider Schuman's proposal as a very important progress in the Franco-German relations, and cannot underline enough its meaning and importance. [...] I declared that the integration of coal, steel and iron would create definitely conditions under which there was no longer any room for any conflict between France and Germany. This is what I felt as the outstanding signification of the decision taken by the French government."[55]

But what Adenauer said in the evening was not yet achieved in the morning, and the morning is not yet over, Mischlich still waits for being entitled to communicate Adenauer's agreement to Schuman, the "decision of the French government" has not yet been taken. In his memoirs, Adenauer does not come back to his conversation with Mischlich, but he gives

---

54 Adenauer, Erinnerungen, op.cit., p. 331.
55 Ibidem.

an account of his meeting with Adenauer, which – at that moment we interrupted the story for a look on what happened on the German side – started at "around 11 a.m., as already quoted from Mischlich's memoirs. Let us remind ourselves that Mischlich arrived at the Chancellor's office at around 9 a.m., the cabinet meeting started at 9.30 a.m., Mischlich met first with Blankenhorn, had to convince that the cabinet meeting must be interrupted, Blankenhorn complied, but discussed Schuman's letters "at length" with Adenauer, which might have taken a large part of the hour between 10 and 11 a.m. ... anyway, Mischlich reached his destiny, the Chancellor in his office, at around 11 – one hour ahead of the deadline imposed by Schuman.

There is "no witness for this meeting. Whether he received somebody in his office, whether he took the floor in any arena – Adenauer was always an event himself. It was after all the third time that I met with the Chancellor – by the way, he very kindly reminded me of these meetings [whereas Adenauer, as we saw, wrote much later in his memoirs that he did not even remember the name of Mischlich] –, but I was still fascinated by this 74-year-old man, whose slender and juvenile appearance impressed me much." Adenauer went straightforward to the crucial issue: "He told me: 'I took notice of the letters you brought and I am still entirely overwhelmed.' He added: 'I fought my whole life through for Franco-German reconciliation and today, thanks to the generous initiative of Robert Schuman, the hope I always had is fulfilled.' This was obviously a great day for this man and I think I perceived that his lips – of him, who usually was so calm disciplined! – slightly trembled and thus showed how deeply and emotionally he was concerned. 'This French proposal, he continued, in historical in any respect; it renders its dignity to my country and is at the same time the cornerstone for the unification of Europe, in which I believe so strongly. [...] Tell your Minister', Adenauer continued, 'that I agree without any reservation and that I will take on the duty to support and defend it whenever necessary.'"[56]

At this point Mischlich inserts one of the very few personal assessments of the people he met and the events he experienced: "Just as Robert

---

56 Mischlich, Mission secrète, op.cit., p. 61.

Schuman, Adenauer was convinced that European unification would only be made possible via Franco-German reconciliation. I could now perceive to which extent these two men were spiritually members of the same family, marked by the same culture, committed to the same values and engaged in the same combat." And Mischlich dares to envisage the big picture: "In reality the Franco-German reconciliation is not born in the Chancellor's offices, its milestones are not outstanding events or treaties; it is much more an outcome of the personal engagement of humans, among them Robert Schuman and Konrad Adenauer in the first place, who had suffered both of them under the Nazi regime."[57]

According to Mischlich's memories, Adenauer was so enthusiastic that he wanted to convoke immediately a press conference and lay open to the large public this plan – now, not only in the evening! Mischlich, "with great deference, pointed to the fact that my Minister himself had the intention to give a public declaration in the evening and that he [Schuman] urgently asked for keeping the secret about the plan, treat it confidentially until this declaration. I added that any indiscretion could made the plan fail, in particular because the French cabinet had not even been acquainted with it. The Chancellor agreed and promised to wait for the French government to make the plan public." 8 p.m., the moment envisaged anyway for the press conference, complied with this promise, because the corresponding event in Paris was scheduled to take place two hours earlier.

It is revealing with regard to the question whether Adenauer really did not know anything about the plan beforehand, what Mischlich remembers at the end of the meeting: "He asked some questions concerning the emergence of the plan. Since I was not among the initiates, I could only tell him what Robert Schuman had told me. My comments on this point must have been rather uncertain and confused. The Chancellor perceived that and did not insist on more information."[58]

---

57 By the way, nobody tells us in his memoirs or comments in which language Adenauer and Mischlich communicated – it can only be German, and Schuman probably chose his compatriot from Lorrain as well for this reason: Mischlich spoke German.
58 Mischlich, Mission secrète, op.cit., p. 62.

Back in Paris: Smalltalk in cabinet,
upheaval in the evening

Mischlich had fulfilled all elements of his mission – but it was high time now! "As soon as I had left the Chancellor's office, I thought that Robert Schuman was sitting in the cabinet meeting at the same time and hurried up to give a telephone call to Bernard Clappier and inform him about the positive reaction of Konrad Adenauer. Bernard Clappier said that he would immediately inform the Minister about our conversation. I had a look on my watch, it was exactly 11.45 a.m. I had respected the deadline my Minister had set."[59]

Very narrowly though ... We change the focus, but ourselves back to Paris and listen to what happened in these minutes in the French cabinet meeting. The 'initiates', Schuman above all, but Clappier too of course, were waiting with growing unease and ever more nervously for the so much hoped-for relief from Bonn. The only one who gives an account of these moments and indeed minutes is Jean Monnet – neither Robert Schuman nor Bernard Clappier, much less one of the French ministers or Georges Bidault himself left any trace in their memoirs of this decisive moment. We listen to Monnet then, who can at least refer himself who could rely on the oral account of Clappier: "The cabinet was meeting in the Elysée Palace and Clappier remembers the long waiting time in a neighboring office. We were connected with Rue de Martignac by an interministerial telephone connection. Noon was over and the agenda had been finished, without Schuman saying a word. He could not take the floor before he was sure that Adenauer did agree, and did agree without reserve, something he was did not doubt, but he needed the information explicitly. This long silence threatened us: Should everything depend on a few minutes? Michlich's [again, Monnet made a mistake in writing his name, even if in French pronunciation it would have sounded correctly ...] message reached Clappier at the moment when the cabinet meeting had just come to a close and everybody was invited to sit down again. What Schuman now told his colleagues will ever be a secret, but I have good reasons to

---

59 Ibidem, p. 63.

believe that he was even more reserved and spoke even less understandably than normally. Nobody questioned the proposal he wanted to take to London, and Pleven as well as Mayer supported it with emphasis, whereas most of the other ministers learned about the precise content only the next morning from the press. After the final end of the cabinet meeting Clappier called me: 'We succeeded, now things can really start.'"[60]

What had happened was nothing less that the decision of the French government to launch the first European Community, for coal and steel. And only one or two hours earlier the German government had taken the same decision to go this way towards European unification. In a dramatic move, France and (West-)Germany had committed themselves to the same, common trajectory for a united Europe.

---

60 Monnet, Mémoires, op.cit., p. 439.

IV The controversy on 9th May

But – was this really as dramatic as I told it here? Did it really depend on a couple of quarters of hours? Did it happen exactly in this way, that morning, 9th May, between 9 a.m. (Mischlich's arrival at the Chancellor's office) and shortly after noon (the formal endorsement by the French government? It might have been all different[61]) the exact chronology of the two days 8th and 9th of May is submitted to an intense controversy.[62] For others – and partly the same! – actors remember a different chronology. One could of course let the matter rest here and turn to the future – at least there is no doubt about what happened until Monday morning and from Tuesday afternoon on; so why a lot of fuss about the 24 hours in-between?

There are two reasons to elucidate precisely the succession of events: On the one hand the question, how exactly decisions of great outreach were taken in both countries, a question crucial for the governance modes in France and Germany at the time, for democracy. Is there a confirmation of the formula that Adenauer was the "Chancellor or lonely decisions"[63]? This would be indeed the case had he been informed only that Tuesday morning, 9th May, as I told the story here, if he did indeed take

---

61 See Mischlich, Mission secrète, a.a.O., preface by Henri Rieben, p. 11: „Le lecteur attentif notera entre les deux récits d'Herbert Blankenhorn et de Robert Mischlich un léger décalage relatif au déroulement de la mission dans le temps. Ce n'est pas notre rôle d'arbitrer. Il y a dans l'histoire de grandes et de petites énigmes. Voici une petite énigme que nous sommes heureux de confier aux historiens, qui, aujourd'hui, de plus en plus nombreux, se penchent avec une science aiguisée et une attention minutieuse sur cette période de notre histoire."

62 Paul Collowald: Die Kontroverse um den 9. Mai 1950. In: Klaus Schwabe (Hrsg.): Konrad Adenauer und Frankreich. Stand und Perspektiven der Forschung zu den deutsch-französischen Beziehungen in Politik, Wirtschaft und Kultur. Bonn 2005 (Rhöndorfer Gespräche Band 21), pp. 82–100.

63 „Kanzler der einsamen Entscheidungen", that is how the journalist Günter Gaus calls the chancellor, referring to a widespread formula of the time, in a half hour long interview with Adenauer, 29th December 1965 in the German TV (ARD); the transcript of the interview is available here: https://www.rbb-online.de/zurperson/interview_archiv/adenauer_konrad.html; Video of the interview here: https://www.youtube.com/watch?v=90EVIH4KZsc

the decision to agree with Schuman's plan spontaneously and without consulting anybody else (except Blankenhorn, maybe), without participation of any other member of his government, left alone any other constitutional body, political party or even public opinion. On the other hand: Had he been informed the day before, he would have had the time to discuss this decision "for Europe" with such far reaching consequences with other leading politicians, ministers, colleagues … And if he did not do anything of the kind anyway, then it would be an additional argument for qualifying him as a maverick.[64] Similar considerations apply to Schuman: Did he get yet any form of agreement from Adenauer beforehand, before the cabinet meeting started that Tuesday morning? Did he push his tactical ruse so far to hold this agreement back throughout the cabinet meeting, intending a final coup and take his colleagues by surprise? Or did he get the message really only in the last moment, when there was not enough time left to explain the plan in detail, when he could invoke the pressure of time as a fig leaf for his rudimentary communication of the project?

On the other hand, it is simply the suspense, like in law court or even a detective story, where witnesses contradict each other – and the observer (as much as the judge …) wants to find out who the "culprit" was …! Und the witnesses! Schuman, Adenauer, Monnet, Clappier, Blankenhorn,

---

64 The Konrad Adenauer Foundation draws the attention to Adenauer's motivations to write his memoirs: "Three motives were decisive. The probably most important one was the intention to rectify the presentation of event, which had been misunderstood by the German public and to underline the true causes and reasons for decisions and evolutions. At the same time he wanted to counter the widespread perception that he had been a chancellor of lonely decisions. A second motivation was Adenauer's desire to explain the fundamental principles of his policy and to demonstrate his long-term aims, like the reunification of Germany, Franco-German reconciliation and the reduction of East-West tensions. He wanted to reconstitute the state of knowledge and insight at the time of his decisions, wanted to perceive them with the same regard as at the original moment, and not with hindsight." https://www.konrad-adenauer.de/dokumente/erinnerungen-adenauers-memoiren; translated for this book by HM. Adenauer took the allegation of taking "lonely decision" seriously – but still does not deny, with regard to 9th May 1950, that he acted accordingly, on the contrary. At the same time his motivation shows that his efforts to give a reliable account, just for such situations, must have been very high.

Mischlich! Their testimonials are obviously not always congruent, but contradictory – and therefore some of them must be wrong. Moreover, some of the witnesses contradict themselves in different sources they left, as e.g. Adenauer! Let us then pursue the investigation and hear the witnesses one by one, especially those who defend an alternative chronology, above all Herbert Blankenhorn, and him first, because he was the only mediator of the meeting between Mischlich and Adenauer in the Chancellor's office, and, additionally, because he was Adenauer's closest advisor, at least in external affairs.[65]

Herbert Blankenhorn, called to the witness stand

Herbert Blankenhorn gives an account of many interesting and important events of the early years of the Federal Republic in his diary. He noted apparently events in a daily rhythm so that there are nearly no doubts about the dates; most of them were written down the same day they had happened – except errors or intended wrong dates. Why Blankenhorn should have done this intendedly in this case, is not at all obvious, but one can never absolutely exclude a mistake. Blankenhorn repeats the same chronology as in his diary in the article he contributed to the book "L'Europe – une longue marche", edited by the Jean Monnet Foundation, under the title of "Herbert Blankenhorn, Ambassadeur de la République fédérale d'Allemagne, témoigne" – meaning that he consciously assumes the role of a witness in this case. In both texts Blankenhorn says that it was 8th May, not 9th, when Mischlich came to Bonn and even indicates two very precise moments for the meetings with him:

- "Bonn, Monday, 8th May 1950
  In the morning at 12 a.m. the collaborator of the French Foreign Minister Schuman, Mister Michlin [sic¡] arrives at my office and wants to hand over to the Chancellor a personal letter of his minister. The letter contains the sensational proposal of the French government to put the

---

65 Herbert Blankenhorn: Verständnis und Verständigung. Blätter eines politischen Tagebuchs 1949–1979. Frankfurt a.M., Berlin, Wien 1980.

French and the German production of coal and steel under a common authority."
- "Afternoon, 6 p.m., reception of Mister Michlin by the Chancellor: handing over of the two responses. One convenes upon the publication of the French move for Tuesday evening, 9th May, as soon as Schuman would have laid open the great news to the world's public in a scheduled press conference."[66]

Three historians refer explicitly to Blankenhorn's account: First of all, Hans-Peter Schwarz in his seminal biography of Adenauer's life. Schwarz follows Blankenhorn without hesitation, but changes the moment of the afternoon meeting, for incomprehensible reasons, from 18.00 o'clock (as Blankenhorn wrote) to 18.50 o'clock (maybe only a typing error?). And he introduces Mischlich with a second given name – Jean – nobody else ever mentioned. These details, as tiny as they maybe, reveal a certain degree of inaccuracy.

Ulrich Lappenküper has put the emergence and the destiny of the Schuman plan under the microscope and decided as well to rely on the account of Blankenhorn, however with the lapidary remark that Mischlich mentioned "erroneously 9th May as the date of his trip to Bonn." Given the very conscious, lively and detailed report Mischlich gave, it is not appropriate to dismiss his chronology as a marginal mistake. And Lappenküper modifies Blankenhorn's indication of Mischlich's arrival – 12 o'clock – into "in the late morning".

Blankenhorn's biographer, Birgit Ramscheid, delivers the most scrupulous analysis of the chronological details in the account of Blankenhorn; however, her statements are the most doubtful ones. Ramscheid says: "Just because of the rather uneasy atmosphere during Schuman's visit [in January], the message, which Robert Mischlich, a collaborator of Schuman, handed over to Blankenhorn was such a surprise in the Chancellery [...] Mischlich's mission was secret; even the French High Commission war not informed beforehand [now follows in Ramscheid's book a footnote: "7th

---

66 Ibidem, p. 100. In his contribution to „L'Europe une longue marche" Blankenhorn repeats this chronology of the events (p. 59 and 62), but writes this time the name of Mischlichs correctly.

May [sic!, i.e. Sunday!] Mischlich applied to Blankenhorn. He [Mischlich] perceived him [Blankenhorn] in this way:" Ramscheid quotes how Mischlich characterized Blankenhorn from Mischlich's memoirs. The date "7th May" is without any doubt a mistake – but if there is a mistake with this date, then the reliability of other dates is uncertain too.

The way in which Ramstein relates the motives and terms relevant for an appropriate assessment of the Schuman plan reveals the fact that Ramstein did not precisely understand what it was really about. "The political essence of the Schuman's offer concerned", in her words, "the economic cooperation between the Federal Republic and France on the basis of equal rights. Additionally, the project of the intergovernmental organization should be open for the participation of other European states. Blankenhorn qualified this proposal as a 'sensational proposal'. 'The Chancellor is convinced that his French move will initiate an entirely new evolution', notes Blankenhorn in his diary. The documents quoted by Ramscheid from Blankenhorn's diary are dated back to 8th May, as we saw already.

In the final analysis, Ramscheid is neither in terms nor in political substance – both are not independent from each other – correct: The "political essence" of the Schuman Plan was just not only "economic cooperation of the basis of equality", but much more peace keeping through the construction of a European Federation beyond national sovereignty; Adenauer himself immediately seized this real signification of the proposal. And that is the reason why it was not about "intergovernmental", but "supranational" organisation, not about a horizontal cooperation between sovereign states, but about the agreement of these states of a political authority beyond themselves, an authority, which would have the legitimacy to take binding decisions for both states (and others which might join). "Intergovernmental" and "supranational" are far from being synonymous, they are contrasting, and should by no means mixed up in such a context.

Whatever the tiniest detail may have been – no doubt that Blankenhorn asserts that he received Mischlich 8th May around noon, that he discussed the plan between this moment and late in the afternoon and that Mischlich got two letters from Adenauer at 6 p.m. At this moment ends the Blankenhorn's contribution to the chronology of events. Above all, there is no notice or any other trace concerning the question whether Mischlich got only the letters or an oral response from Adenauer to the questions raised by Schuman – in this case he would have had the possibility, after 6 p.m., to contact and inform Clappier or Schuman himself about the outcome of mission by telephone. Otherwise, without such an oral confirmation of Adenauer's agreement and only equipped with the two letters in his briefcase but not informed about her content, he would have been obliged to take the night train back to Paris in order to convey the message from Germany on time.

A second inconsistency between Blankenhorn's diary and the real conditions for Mischlich's trip to Bonn is the incompatibility between the moment of arrival around noon on the one hand and the material conditions Mischlich had to reach Bonn. Paul Collowald, later General director of information at the European Union, at that time journalist at the French newspaper "Le monde", asked himself "the very simple question: When would Mischlich have had to leave Paris to arrive at Bonn [around noon]? After a couple of telephone-calls I got a first result: In the year 1953 [sic!] it took eight hours and a half by train from Paris to Cologne, and then another half hour for the connection to Bonn. If we add half an hour for the stay in Cologne, we arrive at nine hours and a half." Additionally he had to make his way from the train station to the Chancellor's office, the Palais Schaumburg, by taxi not much more than ten minutes, but with all the business around certainly some minutes longer, then it took some minutes to get into the office, meet with Blankenhorn ... we all know how easy and indeed inevitable it is in such cases to lose a quarter of an hour.[67] According to Collowald's plausible calculation Mischlich simply had no chance to arrive at Bonn "around noon" – if we assume that Schuman sent him out that Monday morning at 9 a.m. (or even earlier): Mischlich, as we know, reports in detail this moment, his mission, extensively and authentically. He certainly could not have taken a train before 9 or 10 a.m., but then could not arrive earlier than 8 p.m. – too late even for at 6 p.m., but most obviously Adenauer would not have had the time to deliberate with Blankenhorn about the proposal and additionally write two letters.

---

67 Had Schuman put a car at the disposal of Mischlich, he could have made it hardly quicker, as today: Under very good conditions it takes approximately five hours, on fully developed freeways and without border control; in 1950 it would have taken at least twice as much time.

Conclusion of the interrogation with the witness Blankenhorn: His testimony is of captivating precision, diaries are normally reliable sources in such questions of chronology – and still, it is doubtful what he relates, not only because Mischlich, Monnet and Clappier tell the story in a quite different way, but simply because Blankenhorn's chronology is incompatible with the travel conditions of the time.

Bernard Clappier, second witness

Let us call Bernard Clappier to the same witness stand, to some extent the counterpart of Blankenhorn – he was the closest collaborator of Robert Schuman in this field, as Blankenhorn was for Adenauer, and Clappier was involved in the conception and implementation of the plan from the scratch, was therefore very much impressed by the events and should remember them particularly well. He too was invited by the Jean Monnet Foundation to contribute to the volume already referred to, "L'Europe – une longue marche" – by means of an interview ... and his answer to the chronological question make things ever more confusing. When asked "When did Konrad Adenauer get the information?", his answer is: "Very precisely ["très exactement"!] the evening before. 8th May, in the morning, Robert Schuman gave a telephone call to the Chancellor and announced him the visit of a collaborator, who would convey to him a personal letter. This collaborator, Mister Mischlich, arrived late in the afternoon at Bonn and handed the letter of the Minister over to the Chancellor, with an accompanying second letter, explaining the proposal, which was meant to be laid open to the cabinet the next day. Mischlich came back to Paris by night. He brought back the positive answer of the Chancellor."

The next question of the interviewer aimed at 9th May itself: Were there "really fears that there would be difficulties in the cabinet?" Clappier's answer: "Not really. There was a false alarm: Around noon the Ministers seemed to leave, and Schuman had not yet taken the floor. Schuman's message had indeed been scheduled for the end of meeting and that's what he did, between noon and 1 p.m. As far as I can remember the false alarm was in reality only a short break."[68]

---

68 Clappier, Interview in L'Europe une longue marche, op.cit., p. 27.

But how reliable are these memories of Clappier, which – at the difference of Blankenhorn's – are not backed by any diary of other sources of the time when the events took place? It seems as if Clappier sometimes has some doubts himself with regard to the reliability of his own account: "As far as I can remember …" is a sign in kind. Not only has Jean Monnet a different story in mind, in memory, but he remembers even a different story of Clappier's himself, which we should oppose to Clappiers late testimonial: "The cabinet was meeting in the Elysée Palace and Clappier remembers the long waiting time in a neighboring office. We were connected with Rue de Martignac by an inter-ministerial telephone connection. Noon was over and the agenda had been finished, without Schuman saying a word. He could not take the floor before he was sure that Adenauer did agree, and did agree without reserve, something he was did not doubt, but he needed the information explicitly. This long silence threatened us: Should everything depend on a few minutes?" Paul Collowald remembers Clappier being nervous as well: "I knew Bernard Clappier very well. He told me that he, as head of office of the Foreign Minister, waited in an office side by side with the cabinet's meeting room and that he was worried to death, waiting for the telephone call from Bonn."[69] Strange enough, Jean Monnet and Paul Collowald, independently from each other, took notice of Clappier's concerns, which hint, in opposition to his own late testimonial at dramatic and critical moments of the events 9th May! And the fact that Clappier's memories were somewhat unreliable or at least confused became already clear when the nearly equally dramatic scene on the Paris East Station was at stake – for that moment too Clappier's information is contradictory.

Conclusion of the interrogation of Clappier, concerning the choice between 8th and 9th May: He asserts – at the difference of Blankenhorn – that Mischlich must have arrived 8th May, but only in the evening, and that he came back to Paris with the written response of Adenauer during the night. According to this schedule, Adenauer would have had to read and reflect

---

69 Collowald, Kontroverse, op.cit., p. 98. See as well Paul Collowald's account in his memoirs: J'ai vu naître l'Europe. De Strasbourg à Bruxelles, le parcours d'un pionnier de la construction européenne. Strasbourg 2014.

upon the proposal of Schuman in the short time between Mischlich's arrival "late in the afternoon" and his departure in the evening, would have had to discuss the proposal with Blankenhorn, would have had to agree and write (i.e. dictate, let them typewrite, read them again) two letters – a very tight, very improbable schedule! Additionally, Adenauer would have had the opportunity (as according to Blankenhorn's chronology) to inform the German cabinet about the plan – something he did not do –, but would have taken a lonely decision anyway already the evening before and communicated it to Schuman. It rests a secret under these conditions too, why there was so much disquietude that Tuesday morning, why Clappier was so stressed. And in general, Clappier's chronology is questionable in other cases as well.

Konrad Adenauer, called to the witness stand

Strangely, the most confusing testimonial it the one delivered by Konrad Adenauer – the only witness who contradicts himself. I quoted already extensively his memoirs, starting with this sentence concerning 9th May: "In the morning, I did not yet know that this day would become a turning point in the European development" – a remark, which could only mean the arrival of Robert Mischlich and Schuman's proposal, following immediately that introductory sentence. Then Adenauer reports with much accuracy the details of the ensuing events, as already quoted too: ""During the deliberation in the cabinet, I got the information that a special envoy of the French Foreign Minister Schuman wanted to communicate an important message to me personally. Assistant Secretary of State Blankenhorn received the man, who handed over to him two letters of Schuman. […] Blankenhorn handed both letters over to me in the cabinet room." If there were no other sources, these memories would not leave any room for a different chronology, because they are so authentic and accurate, and coincide perfectly with Mischlich's. But the fact is that there are other sources, left by Adenauer himself, which inevitable revive just these doubts: Nothing less than the two letters written by the Chancellor as his answer to Schuman's two letters, the official and the personal one: These two letters, which Mischlich had to take back to Paris, are dated Monday, 8th May! Additionally, in these letters Adenauer tells Schuman that the

German cabinet would take its decision about joining the Council of Europe "tomorrow".[70]

Hans-Peter Mensing, editor of Adenauer's letters, additionally points to another source: "The timetable of the chancellor and the lists of visitors [...] confirm without any doubt that he received 'Mister Mischlich, French High Commission, on Monday, 8th May, 18.50 o'clock'".[71] However, there is at least one mistake in this notice: Mischlich was just not a member of the French High Commission, he had been sent by Schuman himself in order to circumvent the High Commission's involvement. And the indication of the time – 18.50 o'clock – differs at least nearly one hour from Blankenhorn's, who dated the visit of Mischlich at 18.00 o'clock. Finally, this visit, according to Blankenhorn, was already the second one, whereas there is apparently no proof of the same kind for Mischlich's first visit (if it ever took place ...).

Notwithstanding these doubts, Hanns Jürgen Küsters has found a further source, which hints at 8th May as the day of Mischlich's arrival: "During my search for the detailed circumstances [...] I found a remark of Adenauer from 26th March 1953 [...] Adenauer commented on these events face to the foreign affairs committee of the German Federal Council [the parliamentary chamber of representatives of the German regions]: 'I asked to pick up a letter from Schuman from 7th May 1950 ...' He then gave an account of the content and finally referred to his motives. There, he says something decisive: 'And therefore, because I was on the same line from

---

70 Hans Peter Mensing in his contribution to the discussion with Collowald: Die Kontroverse um den 9. Mai, op.cit., S. 94, with reference to: Adenauer, Briefe 1949–1951, edited by Rudolf Morsey und Hans Peter Schwarz, bearbeitet von Hans Peter Mensing. Berlin 1985, p. 208, pp. 508–510; see as well Akten zur Auswärtigen Politik der Bundesrepublik Deutschland 1949/50, bearbeitet von Daniel Kosthorst und Michael F. Feldkamp. München 1997, S. 145–147. How easily mistakes occur in dating back historical sources is shown by the otherwise very reliable online archive of CVCE, where this letter is translated into French, calls the French version "original", announces it as a letter from 8th May and inserts in the text the date "9th May"! https://www.cvce.eu/de/obj/reponse_personnelle_de_konrad_adenauer_a_robert_schuman_bonn_8_mai_1950-fr-4e096ce7-343a-473f-9458-579f627e2ec7.html.
71 Collowald, op.cit, p. 94.

the beginning, I immediately, the same evening, when I received this letter [from Schuman], I sat down and conferred a letter to the man [i.e. Mischlich], where I with welcomed this move with all my conviction.' Adenauer confirmed three years later that he handed the letter over that evening."[72]

Obviously a dilemma – Adenauer's memoirs are the work of a statesman, who carefully relates his political life day by day, and other mistakes in chronological dating of events did apparently not occur. This event in particular, which had such an overwhelming importance for Adenauer, has certainly not been dealt with at the margins, incidentally, casually, as something, which did not require accuracy in detail – the testimonial of the memoirs must be taken seriously. But dating letters wrong? Can such a mistake happen? Or is one of both versions intentionally wrong, should Adenauer have dated the letters, written 9th May, back to the day before? Or should he have been mistaken in his memoirs, despite his best will to be accurate? But if we assume the last case – wrong chronology in the memoirs – then not only the date of Mischlich's messaging would be wrong, but the whole coherent series of events must be wrong. The whole series of events cannot have taken place on Monday, 8th May – the cabinet meeting, when Germany's membership in the Council of Europe was on the agenda, took place on Tuesday, 9th May, without any doubt. Both events – deliberations in cabinet on Council of Europe and Mischlich's visit – are so closely interwoven that it is difficult to believe that one of both would be wrong. And the letters, dated to 8th May? Paul Collowald, decidedly in favour of Mischlich's Chronology, gives several examples of mistaken dating in seemingly reliable sources, to illustrate the possibility that this could have happened as well in the case under scrutiny here.

A closer look on the two letters Adenauer wrote reveals that they had no unequivocal destiny. Adenauer himself did apparently no longer dispose of the (copies of) his own original letters, at least not of the second, the personal one. From this fact, Hans Peter Mensing draws the argument that Adenauer, when writing his memoirs, did no longer have his letters at hand, which would have allowed him to correctly date the events according to the dates of the letters (i.e., in Mensing's opinion, 8th May). For

---

72 Küster's contribution to Collowald, Kontroverse, op.cit., p. 96.

this argument Mensing relies on Adenauer's last letter to Robert Schuman, 24th July 1963, where he writes: "This letter, which launched such a decisive evolution for our two nations, is unfortunately lost to me." Mensing interrupts the quotation and comments: "Only in 1985, in the Rhöndorf edition [of Adenauer's letters] did we decide to include this *missing link* in the correspondence." Then Mensing continues quoting Adenauer's own words: "It would probably be kept in some file in the Foreign Office," (Mensing adds: "Right, this is where Mister Küsters found the letter"), where it could not find it despite intense research. Therefore, I would like to ask you, dear colleague, to send me a copy of your handwritten letter of that moment, if you could do that."[73] But obviously Adenauer is no longer talking here about *his own*, but of Schuman's letter (dated, as we see, to 7th May, what does not mean much); Mensing mixes up Adenauer's own with Schuman's letter; and the letter, which Hanns Jürgen Küsters found and published in the collection of Adenauer's correspondence in 1985, was not the one Adenauer refers to in his letter to Schuman from 1963, but was Adenauer's *own one*. However, curious enough, even this letter seems to have been lost, otherwise Küsters and Mensing would not have qualified it as a unexpected finding.

And Paul Collowald confirms that Adenauer's letter had a strange periplus, before surfacing as a historical source: Collowald was "hugely surprised when I say the text of this letter [meaning probably the letter itself] in a showcase of an exposition in Brussels organized at the occasion of the 30th anniversary of the Rome Treaties. [...] Suddenly I discovered a document (number 23), related to the category 'The Schuman Plan', with this explanation: 'handwritten letter from Adenauer, 8th May 1950 (day before the Schuman declaration). Private collection.' I had a closer look and found out that at the end of the German text – I knew the French translation, published in Lausanne [in the quoted book "L'Europe une longue marche"] – there was an additional sentence added by the Chancellor himself: 'I shall be happy when these ideas, which I pursued since 1925, will become reality.'" But Collowald immediately asked himself: "What does private collection mean? Who owned this document?"

---

73 Mensing's comment on Collowald, ibidem, p. 94.

Konrad Adenauer, called to the witness stand 77

He finds out that it was a German colleague in the European Commission, at the time when Walter Hallstein was its president, Nikolaus von Mach, who tells Collowald that he discovered "in early 1965 in the 'Frankfurter Allgemeine Zeitung', that there were handwritten documents on sale, in Paris, in the Galerie Drouot, documents from famous people, addressed to Robert Schuman, which he had collected and which now would be sold of by auction. You probably know that he was not married and that his heirs had the unfortunate idea to sell the bounty." Collowald revealed that the letter published by Blankenhorn in "L'Europe, une longue marche" had "not that handwritten additional sentence of the Chancellor. The orgininal, however, with the added sentence of the Chancellor, has been published in the beautiful volume 'Un changement d'espérance'. [...] That is what Hanns Jürgen Küsters already indicated in his contribution to the book 'Die Anfänge des Schuman-Plans [the origins of the Schuman plan] in a footnote."[74] Which letter did Küster and Mensing found in the archive of the Foreign Office, for their 1985 edition of Adenauer's correspondence – if Collowald found the original two years after this edition in an exposition showing private property?! Obviously 'only' a copy, as Küsters admits himself: "Adenauer's handwritten additional remark from was lacking on this copy. The copy itself was filed in the department 200 of the Foreign Office. That was the department concerned with European fundamental questions. This is the literal text published in the 'Rhöndorfer Ausgabe'".[75]

This maybe overdetailed analysis of everything Adenauer left leads to the following conclusion:

- Both of his letters are dated 8th May.
- Three years later, Adenauer confirms in the Federal Council that he had been informed 8th May.

---

74 Collowald, Kontroverse, op,cit., p. 87. The reference is: Un changement d'espérance. La Déclaration du 9 mai 1950. Jean Monnet – Robert Schuman. Edited by Fondation Jean Monnet pour l'Europe, Lausanne 2000. Hanns Jürgen Küsters footnote in: Küsters.: Die Verhandlungen über das institutionelle System zur Gründung der Europäischen Gemeinschaft für Kohle und Stahl. In: Schwabe (ed.), Die Anfänge des Schuman-Plans, op.cit., pp. 73–102, here p. 77.
75 Küsters in Collowald, Kontroverse, op.cit., p. 99.

- Agenda and list of visitors of the Chancellor confirm equally 8th May as the day of Mischlich's visit.
- On the other hand, his memoirs decidedly confirm that it was 9th May, when Mischlich informed Adenauer, and integrate this event with the cabinet meeting dedicated to the question of the Federal Republic's membership in the Council of Europe, a cabinet meeting which certainly took place that 9th May.

Robert Schuman, called to the witness stand

As already mentioned, Robert Schuman did not leave any memoirs and his legacy has been flogged by his heirs to a large extent, so that there are only a few documents available, and by chance – as for instance Adenauer's letter with his handwritten additional remark, discovered by Paul Collowald in an exposition. Schuman's only own contribution to the "controversy about 9th May" is therefore a statement he gave three years after the events, 22nd and 23rd October 1953, in two speeches he gave when the Robert Schuman chair was inaugurated at the College of Bruges and at the invitation of the first rector of the College, Henri Brugmans, himself one of the outstanding intellectuals of the time and protagonist of a federal unification of Europe.[76] But at that occasion Schuman mentions only incidentally that he had informed Adenauer 8th May: "Twenty-four hours before 9th May the allied governments, as well as the German government, got the information. Before we dropped the bombshell, we had to make sure how the most important partners would receive the message. For us the decisive partner [...] was the German Federal government, and that is why we asked for the general agreement of the Chancellor. The other

---

76 Hendrik Brugmans, one of the outstanding European intellectuals of the middle of the century, left two autobiographic books, which allow for very lively insights in the experiences of his generation. They in particular make the European consequences plausible which he himself as much as many others draw from these experiences: L'Europe vécu. Brussels 1979, and À travers le siècle. Brussels 1993. The latter contains one of the very few testimonies of the meeting of European federalists at Hertenstein, where the "Charter of Hertenstein" was laid down, as will later be discussed.

governments, the British, Italian, American, the Benelux-countries were informed twenty-four hours before the declaration."[77]

This is another information as inaccurate as improbable in to some extent certainly untrue account: The other governments were not informed at all[78] and Schuman is not explicit as to the order in which the Chancellor (first?) and then the other (who) governments got the message about the French initiative – only Acheson (together with Bruce), i.e. the American government, had been informed beforehand, as already mentioned, on Sunday, 7th May. Furthermore, Schuman does not indicate in which way (by telephone, in written form, via personal envoys, diplomatic channels or else) the information war spread in his marginal mention of the events. After all it was under the spell of absolute secrecy that he treated the plan until he got the Adenauer's and the French government's agreement – and that happened without any doubt only Tuesday, 9th May. The late and vague information Schuman gave at the College of Bruges is, compared to the explicit and detailed sources at hand too unreliable to sustain the hypotheses that the Chancellor had been informed 8th and not 9th May.

---

77 Discours de Robert Schuman sur les origines et sur l'élaboration de la CECA (Bruges, 22–23 octobre 1953): „Vingt-quatre heures avant le 9 mai, les gouvernements alliés et amis, ainsi que le gouvernement fédéral allemand, ont été mis au courant. Nous devions, avant de lancer cette bombe, savoir quel accueil elle recevrait de la part des principaux interlocuteurs. Pour nous, le principal interlocuteur, pour les raisons que j'ai rappelées tout à l'heure, c'était le Gouvernement Fédéral, et c'est ainsi que nous nous sommes assurés avant le 9 mai de l'accord de principe du chancelier fédéral. Les autres gouvernements, britannique, italien, américain ceux du Benelux ont été mis au courant 24 heures avant la proclamation." https://www.cvce.eu/content/publication/2009/3/4/91c347fc-ab32-4e8d-a31f-f8e244362705/publishable_fr.pdf; zuerst in: Collège d'Europe: Cahiers de Bruges. Décembre 1953.

78 This is a certitude Vincent Dujardin cannot put into question, when he questions hints oft he Belgian Minister of economy of the time, who pretends to remember that the Benelux countries, or at least some of their ministers, were informed about Schuman's plan at the occasion of a meeting in Paris, 8th May, exclusively convened to this purpose. See Vincent Dujardin: Mai 1950: le Plan Schuman, l'Allemagne prévenue après le Benelux? In: European Review of History; Revue euroéenne d'Histoire, Vol. 8, No. 1, 2001, pp. 63–66.

Telephone calls

Finally, we might raise the question whether telephone calls did play a role in transmitting the message, as well concerning Adenauer as Schuman. Clappier – but as we see the reliability of his memories is weak – talks about such a telephone call: "Schuman called Adenauer by telephone in the morning of 8th May to announce him the arrival at Bonn of one of his collaborators, mandated to hand over to him a personal message."[79] But this alleged telephone call did not leave any trace neither in Adenauer's nor in Blankenhorn's or Mischlich's diaries or memoirs. Probably, it did not even take place, because Mischlich had certainly relied on such an announcement of his arrival, since it would have largely facilitated his entry in the Chancellor's office and his contact with Blankenhorn.

Hans-Peter Schwarz relates a second telephone call in his biography on Adenauer, after telling the story of the turbulent and conflictual cabinet meeting that Tuesday, 9th May, morning, as far as it can be reconstructed on the basis of the few notes taken by the actors and observers of the moment. As far as the cabinet's decision to accept the invitation to join the Council of Europe is concerned, Schwarz writes: "Now Blankenhorn calls Paris and reports the positive outcome of the cabinet meeting. Soon Adenauer is informed that everything went well with the Schuman plan too."[80] Schwarz does not give any proof of the telephone call, there is no echo of it neither in Blankenhorn' diary nor in his account in "L'Europe, une longue marche". Indeed, it would have been very strange if Blankenhorn would have given priority to the Council of Europe issue, at a moment when the so much more important Schuman plan was at stake. And whom could he have called if not Clappier, his counterpart? But Clappier does not say a word about the call neither.

The third telephone call – if the two before-mentioned have ever taken place – has already been noted: That is the call Mischlich gave to Clappier, 9th May shortly before 11.45 a.m. (when Mischlich, as we saw, had a look on his watch and observed with relief that he had respected Schuman's

---

79 Interview Clappier, in: L'Europe une longue marche, op.cit., p. 26.
80 Hans-Peter Schwarz: Adenauer Der Aufstieg 1876–1952. Stuttgart, Deutsche Verlagsanstalt p. 714.

deadline). This is the telephone call, which lifted Schuman's and Clappier's anxiety about the German reaction and enabled them the put the plan forward in the French government and get its endorsement. But whether this telephone call really take place, whether Mischlich's chronology is accurate is another open question, as we saw, since other sources put it into question. And Mischlich, as we will see, mentions an additional telephone call himself, though less important.

Stoppage time: Mischlich's return to Paris

Finally, one may ask the question what Mischlich did when he had fulfilled his function. Sure, his historical role was over at the same moment, but there might be some evidence concerning the question when precisely his mission was over. Let us listen first to himself again: "When I took my leave from Konrad Adenauer, he asked me very politely whether hu could do anything else for my convenience. 'Yes, indeed, Chancellor', I replied, 'you could help me to disappear without the High Commission in Bonn taking notice, since they are not informed about my mission.' He was highly amused by my considerations since he was very much inclined himself to secret diplomacy. 'I shall put a driver and a car at your disposal and you can make a relaxed trip through our beautiful environment.' He asked me too: 'Do you know Cologne?' Since I negated, he recommended warmly 'his' city, where he had been mayor for so long a time.' On his sightseeing tour, Mischlich enjoys the 'majestic Rhine', the 'peaceful landscapes full of spring flowers' and does not forget to mention: 'It was 9th May and nature was more beautiful than ever.'" But Mischlich returned to the Chancellor's office – to look for the letters, where Adenauer not only orally, but in due written form, officially and personally, gave his own agreement and the agreement of his government to Schuman's plan. If Mischlich did really left the Chancellor's office, as he tells it with so much authenticity, 9th May just before noon, in a governmental car and took the time to visit the (largely destroyed) city of Cologne as well as the "majestic Rhine", then he could not have been back earlier than in the middle, more probably in the late afternoon at the Palais Schaumburg, taking with him Adenauer's letters.

Anyway and according to Mischlich's chronology, it is clear that Schuman relied exclusively on the oral message he had gotten from his special envoy, transmitted by Clappier, when he pushed the plan through in the French cabinet – he did not yet dispose of the written confirmation. According to Mischlich's memoirs he could not even hand Adenauer's letters over to his minister before he had to leave for London, early next morning: "Back to Paris, I could not convey the two letters addressed to him by the Chancellor to Foreign Minister Schuman. The Minister, together with Bernard Clappier, were already in London, attending the Franco-British-American conference."[81] This is another remark important for the chronology of events, even if it is only marginal for the success of his mission.

Clappier, on the other hand, reports that "Mischlich came back in the night" – but Clappier is talking about the night before, from 8th to 9th May ... – and adds: "He brought back with him the Chancellor's positive answer."[82] Besides the previously stated uncertainty of Clappier's memories, it is his intention in this context to make sure that nobody got any information about the plan *before 8th May*. "I am absolutely sure that nothing of what emerged from the Rue de Martignac [Monnet's office] reached Bonn." Taking into account that Clappier does not pay attention to the precise date, left alone the hour, of Mischlich's return to Paris, his statement that he, Mischlich, came back "in the night" sounds ever more uncertain. Additionally, Clappier invalidates his own statement when he tells Monnet and Collowald how nervous he was during the next morning, waiting desperately for the answer from Bonn – had Mischlich come back "in the night", Clappier would have been able to lay back and relax."[83]

Armand Bérard called to the witness stand

A marginal remark so far unnoticed in Mischlich's memoirs could be the key to unravel the mystery: "Bevor I went back to Paris", Mischlich

---

81 Mischlich, Mission secrète, op.cit., p. 64.
82 L'Europe, une longue marche, op.cit., p. 27.
83 Neither Blankenhorn nor Adenauer say anything about Mischlich's return to Paris.

writes, "I gave a telephone call to Armand Bérard, our Deputy High Commissioner to Germany, and informed him succinctly about my mission. Since nobody in the High Commission was aware of my presence in Bonn, I felt obliged on behalf of courtesy to salute him before leaving German territory, even if it was only by telephone. Anyway, there was no provocation or impropriety in such a move. I think Armand Bérard understood it indeed as I meant it."[84] If this telephone call had left an echo in the memoirs of Armand Bérard then one would possibly be able to date it back to the precise moment when Mischlich left Bonn – already in the evening of 8th May, coming back to Paris "in the night", or only in the late afternoon of 9th May, too late to hand the letters over to Schuman before he had to leave for London?

Armand Bérard did indeed leave his memoirs and diaries, in three voluminous books, tracing his fascinating diplomatic parcours over Berlin before the war, Washington and then Bonn (more precisely Remagen and Koblenz, siege of the French High Commission). What is more, he really noted in his diary a telephone call he got from Mischlich – and still, it is just with this notice that the hope of elucidating the mystery of the chronology fades away: "Tuesday, 9th May [...] Mischlich called me before he returned to Paris. He had met the Chancellor again this morning, who handed over to him two letters, one personal and one official, addressed to Schuman. In the High Commission nobody was informed about his presence in Bonn." At least one detail is no longer unclear then: Mischlich's return to Paris can be dated precisely now, with high probability, since Bérard's account coincides with his own – he went back in the afternoon or evening of 9th May and could then not arrive in Pris earlier than in the morning of 10th May; too late for him to convey Adenauer's letters to Schuman personally, who was already underway to London.

On the other hand, the much more important question when Mischlich had met with Adenauer and when he had gotten his agreement becomes ever more confusing: Mischlich had seen the Chancellor *"again"*, says Bérard (in the French original: "Il a revu ce matin le chancelier"), in the morning of 9th May – but then, when did he met him for the first time?

---

84 Mischlich, Mission secrète, op.cit., p. 64.

The day before? The confusion increases if we take into consideration Bérard's other remarks concerning the issue – he asserts that he had been in Paris the day before and had been informed by Clappier about Schuman's Plan: "Monday, 8th May. Before I left Paris, Clappier informed me about the declaration Schuman intended to give in the evening of the following day about his project to put the French and the German coal and steel industry under one common authority. Acheson, who had been informed this morning, after a moment of hesitation, was enthusiastic. Baudet, our deputy state secretary ["ministre conseiller"] in London, has been called back to Paris this evening; he had received the text of the declaration, which he will hand over to Bevin, tomorrow morning, together with Massigli. Ich myself take a text with me, which will be amended tomorrow just before the cabinet meeting and which I keep ready for the Chancellor. Clappier had already told me about the project, which Jean Monnet was about the conceive, a month and a half before." That comes indeed as a big surprise, because until now it was taken for granted that in the High Commission not only Mischlich's mission, but the whole plan was completely unknown.

And Bérard adds further details to the succession of events: 9th May, "back [from Paris] in Remagen [his official residence, some 20 km away from Bonn] I call Clappier around noon. He had promised the official text for 5 o'clock and agrees that I convene a press conference at the same time as Schuman." After Mischlich's telephone call "I summoned Blankenhorn for 3 p.m. He tells me that the Chancellor is entirely happy. In addition to his two letters he had just sent another telegram to Schuman. Blankenhorn asked Mischlich immediately whether Dreesen was informed. When he negated, Adenauer drew the conclusion that it was a personal initiative taken by Schuman and directed to him personally – a triumph of politics over diplomacy: It was then the Quai d'Orsay [i.e. the French diplomacy, not Schuman himself!] who was responsible for all the tensions of the last weeks. In the end the Chancellor was right with this strategy of permanent requirement and protests, since the outcome was now what it was. Blankenhorn asked me to hold my press conference not earlier than Adenauer's. He wanted to have the privilege to inform the German public about the news. He asks me to convey the Schuman declaration to him as soon as I get the text. He delays his press conference to have the opportunity to use the definite text. I agree and cancel the press conference I convened for 18.30 p.m. Besides that, I should have insisted on the fact that the project was an offer to the entire German people without prejudice and party affiliation, and not to the German chancellor personally. But it would have been inappropriate to freeze his enthusiasm and provoke new clouds in this bright atmosphere."[85]

There is no way to admit that Bérard opens an entirely new, his own chronology of the events around 8th and 9th May, different from all the others. If Mischlich had met with the Chancellor *again* in the morning of 9th May to receive his letters to Schuman, then this implies that he had met with him already the day before, telling him what his mission was all about. Bérards notes are not precise about the moment when Mischlich got Adenauer's oral answer, ready to be reported to Paris immediately – either at the first meeting 8th May or only when he received the letters 9th May. However, Bérard's divergent chronology depends entirely on one word: "again". Altogether new is Bérard's assertion that he himself, but then the High Commission as such, as an institution, would have been informed even earlier than Adenauer was by Mischlich.

Conclusion of the inquiry

It is all very unsatisfactory: After so many conflicting testimonies, no unequivocal conclusion can be drawn – whether the information about the plan reached Adenauer on the 8th or 9th May, whether Schuman got the news from Bonn before or only at the end of the cabinet meeting, these

---

85 Armand Bérard: Un ambassadeur se souvient. Washington et Bonn. 1945–1955. Paris 1978, S. 312f. In the first volume of his memoirs (Au temps du danger allemand) Bérard talks about his time in Nazi-Germany, other volumes concern his stays in Rome and Japan. Bérard was a highly estimated and high-ranking diplomat – alongside, not under André François-Poncet, his boss, who was High Commissioner himself. There is not mention of the strange fact that Mischlich did not call François-Poncet himself – who would be very disappointed and furious, when he learned much later about all the events around the Schuman plan –, but Bérard, and why it was Bérard who called Blankenhorn, held the press conference etc. Anyway, it is highly probable that François-Poncet himself was neither in Bonn/Remagen nor in Paris these days.

and other questions must be left open, without any definite answers even today, despite so many sources and witnesses. Blankenhorn's diary and the date on Adenauer's letters, if we put aside Schuman's own (marginal) account, represent the strongest arguments in favour of the earlier chronology – on the other hand, Adenauer's memoirs, Jean Monnet's and in particular Mischlich's very detailed report, plead for the narrower timescale. Clappier's uncertain recollections and Bérard's somewhat vaguer/ambiguous information are not convincing enough to resolve the question. But one of the chronologies must be wrong!

If the hypothesis "9th May" is correct, then both Blankenhorn and Adenauer would have had to have made the same dating error when dating their diary entries and letters (,) respectively – it is highly unlikely that such a coincidence of errors could occur, but it cannot be completely ruled out. Or could it be that they consciously chose the wrong date, 8th May, and if so, why should they have wanted to deceive the public? One motive could have been – and that same motivation seems even plausible for Schuman's remark three years later in Bruges – to give the impression that the communication and decision making surrounding this momentous issue was less dramatic, less improvised, more professional, better planned, more orderly, more in line with diplomatic rules of behaviour. To inform the Chancellor only at the last minute, to let everything depend on one decisive short moment, to risk the failure of the whole project if one telephone call in the last quarter of an hour hadn't been made, all that might have been perceived as an irresponsible, all-or-nothing gamble. Adenauer, as well as Schuman, may have wished to project a more serious, more responsible historical picture of their actions by backdating those decisive steps, starting with Schuman dating his letter to Adenauer as the 7th May. It is conceivable, of course. that this motivation explains the backdating of Adenauer's letters, whereas Blankenhorn may simply have made a mistake in his diary. One piece of evidence for this hypothesis could be the fact that Mischlich could simply not have arrived at the Chancellor's office at the time Blankenhorn remembered. His diary entry is simply incompatible with the material, the physical possibilities that Mischlich had. And it is not quite clear when exactly Blankenhorn noted the events in this diary; the text reads like a summary review– after a couple of days? ... or weeks? Armand Bérard, who was in a comparable situation, leaving similar notes, is the only one in the French diplomatic service to report on ex ante (advance) information about Schuman's coup, could have clarified the question; but his recollections give only precise details concerning Mischlich's departure back to Paris – early afternoon on the 9th May, before 3 p.m., at least. At least it can be said that the "May 8. hypothesis" " is supported precisely by those witnesses who, for diplomatic reasons, may have had an interest in making the whole process look a little more professional, to insist on this more orderly procedure, whereas those who were not bound by such considerations – Monnet, Mischlich, even Adenauer – after he was retired and distanced from his Chancellor's duties – support the "May 9. hypothesis" ".

However, should the "May 8. hypothesis" be the correct version of events, then the memoirs of Adenauer, as well as those of Monnet and Mischlich – which are independent from each other – must all be wrong. Adenauer refers only briefly to the appearance of Mischlich, but in very succinct terms: Is it conceivable that he is mistaken at such a moment(,) of historical significance? – the moment when Germany`s decision about becoming a member of the Council of Europe was at stake, a moment of such paramount importance to him, both emotionally and politically! All the more so since both events – the decision about membership of the Council of Europe and the Schuman Plan – are so closely linked? "In the morning, I did not yet know that this day would become a turning point in European development", writes Adenauer, and continues: "During the deliberations in the cabinet, I was informed that a special envoy of the French Foreign Minister, Schuman, wanted to communicate an important message to me personally." A very precise account of the succession of events, which coincides in every detail with Mischlich's, whose memory of this exceptional moment in his career and life is so detailed and sounds so authentic that it would indeed come as big surprise if he had invented the whole story. If it is a fake, against all the evidence, then Mischlich cannot simply be mistaken; his story is far too rich in minutiae, in atmospheric and practical detail – he would have to have invented it with a truly poetic imagination, had he deliberately thought up the whole of this lively account. Still, could he have been motivated to do so? Could it have been his wish to be seen as the "James Bond of French diplomacy", to take on a more important share in history than he had in real life? And what if

Adenauer made a mistake in his memoirs after all, despite the importance of the issue? But even if these assumptions are right, there are still the Jean Monnet's memoirs to consider, who was also very close to the events, at a moment which was decisive and extremely important for himself as well, at that moment on May at quarter to 12, when Mischlich's telephone call reached Clappier ...?

Both narratives, taken separately, seem to be authentic, convincing and undeniable – if they were not challenged by equally authentic and convincing counterstatements: a real dilemma! Is there any method to resolve it? Are there other sources which could help to decide the issue? Can Adenauer's letters be analysed by means of modern technical devices, through criminology, so to say? Is there any evidence of other chronological mistakes in Blankenhorn's diary(,) which would cast doubt on the reliability of those taken into account here? Mischlich's memoirs are unique, there aren't any others we could compare with this story of the 8th and 9th May 1950. Did other people from that time leave other reports, accounts, testimonies, witnesses often neglected – like secretaries such as Suzanne Miguez for example, Jean Monnet's secretary, who knew the plan of course (after repeatedly typewriting the text, at least nine times)? Adenauer's secretary must have typewritten his answers to Schuman – did she remember the date? Did she remember any advice to date the letters back to the 8th May ...? But nobody seems to have left any testimony of those moments.[86]

---

[86] At the difference of Hannelore Siegel and in particular Anneliese Poppinga; see for later years of Andenauer's chancellorship Anneliese Poppinga: Meine Erinnerungen an Konrad Adenauer. Gütersloh 1970. Hannelore Siegel left some anecdotical memories of Adenauer, which reveal his methods and communicative behaovior: „Adenauer sei ‚als Chef gar nicht kompliziert gewesen', sagte Hannelore Siegel [Adenauers Sekretärin von 1958 bis 1963] der ‚Bild am Sonntag'. So habe er ihr Briefe nicht diktiert sondern nur Stichworte gesagt mit den Worten: ‚Sie können schreiben, wat Se wollen, Frollein Siegel, aber bevor Se dä Sinn ändern, dann frachen Se mich.'"
https://rp-online.de/panorama/deutschland/adenauer-konnte-ein-fieser-moepp-sein_aid-14175123, Rheinische Post online, 29th July 2012, what means in short that he often gave only headwords and left the precise formulation to his secretary, and required only to be informed when she changed the meaning ... But he would probably not have been as casual with his letters to Schuman. Anyway, his private secretary (was she, as *private* secretary, charged with the

Finally, the German cabinet meeting on 9th May must be put under the microscope. According to Hans-Peter Schwarz, only Blankenhorn and Hans-Christoph Seebohm, Minister of transport, left notes from the meeting. Seebohm in particular remembers that the debate in cabinet on that day was turbulent [87], that two other ministers, Jakob Kaiser and Gustav Heinemann (later President of the Federal Republic) opposed the Chancellor's plea for Germany's membership in the Council of Europe; their dispute was so intense that the ministers withdrew for a separate deliberation."[88] Could this have been the window of opportunity for Mischlich's request to interrupt the cabinet meeting? This interruption complies exactly with Mischlich's account of the morning, it makes both accounts compatible, the one on the cabinet meeting and Mischlich's account, it makes Mischlich's improbable success in suspending the cabinet meeting much more plausible – there was simply no need to interrupt the meeting at his request(,) because it had been interrupted anyway(,) because Kaiser and Heinemann wanted to consult separately.

At any rate, not a word about the Schuman plan that morning in cabinet – despite the fact that "Europe" was the big issue/topic of discussion. Is it conceivable that Adenauer had known about the plan since the previous day, that he had already given his written consent – and that he nevertheless made no mention of it during the whole meeting, despite the controversy emerging among his ministers? The information about Schuman's plan could have substantially backed and justified his own position concerning Germany's membership in the Council of Europe, since this plan refuted the decisive argument against it, i.e. the uncertain future of the Saar.[89] Would Adenauer not have used this strong argument in order

---

correspondence with Schuman?) did not leavy any evidence of such things. See Schwarz, Adenauer, op.cit., p. 799.
87 Blankenhorn only talks about a "lengthy exchange of considerations" (a "längerer Gedankenaustausch"); see Blankenhorn, Verständnis und Verständigung, op.cit., p. 102.
88 Schwarz, Adenauer, op.cit., p. 741.
89 That is how Schuman saw things himself. When Mischlich asked him what he should say if Adenauer would raise the question of the Saar region, Schuman replied that he – Adenauer – would certainly not do that. See Mischlich, Mission secrète, op.cit., p. 59.

to settle the dispute to his own advantage? The fact that he did not use this argument is another sign (though not proof!) to back the hypothesis that he received the information about the plan only during, and not before, the cabinet meeting on May 9th. It seems plausible that the remaining time, after his personal talk with Mischlich, was too short to discuss this brand-new issue, all the more so since, according to Seebohm's recollections, Kaiser and Heinemann had aligned themselves behind the Chancellor and agreed on Germany's accession to the Council of Europe.

Similar considerations apply to Schuman, even if in his case the evidence for the more dramatic, " May 9th hypothesis" are not quite as clear. It may simply have been a tactical move to talk about the plan only at the very end of the cabinet meeting – there had already been a fair amount of (political) manoevering/intrigue before then. But still: Had Schuman known about Adenauer's reaction the evening before, the cabinet meeting would have ended in an orderly fashion – there would be no reason for Monnet and Clappier to be anxious and nervous, nor for the mysterious false alarm and the inexplicable pause around noon, according to Clappier's (uncertain) memories, and the delayed agreement on the Schuman's proposal. Are there notes from other ministers about this cabinet meeting, as was the case with their German counterparts? Until now, there is no mention anywhere of such sources. Are there other hidden testimonies in the archives of the French Foreign Ministry, the lost memories of secretaries, train tickets left by Mischlich, a travel expense report accounting for his voyage to Bonn ...? Something of the kind would be sensational, but no administration would guard and store such marginal information in its archives.

The fact is – for the time being – there is no definite answer to the question as to which of the two chronologies – 8th or 9th May – is the right one.[90] However, taking everything into account, after weighing the pros and cons, there is, paradoxically, more to be said in favour of the improbable, the dramatic "May 9th hypothesis", precisely because it is so

---

90 Küsters attempt to harmonize contradictory versions of the story; see Collowald, Kontroverse, op.cit., p. 95.

dramatic and diplomatically risky – this being exactly the reason for some of the main actors to cover it up.

V Schuman's speech

(Anyway) Whatever the case, the time had come for Schuman to declare his plan for a European Coal and Steel Community in the Foreign Ministry's prestigious "Salle d'Horloge" in front of a crowd of journalists. Utmost priority was given to peace – the first word of the declaration is "la paix", peace. That was the ultimate aim, peace keeping, everything else was to work towards this aim.[91] This goal was repeatedly emphasised by Schuman and Monnet from the very start, first of all in their communication with Adenauer, who entirely shared this interpretation of the plan.

The second idea in the speech concerns the method: Europe was to be unified step by step, gradually, and not in all fields at the same time: "Europe will not be created in one fell swoop, or according to a single plan. It will be built through concrete achievements which first create a de facto solidarity." This was the lesson drawn from the failed big-bang projects advanced immediately after the War – Churchill's plan for the United States of Europe, the projects of the European Federalists for a pan-European federation. They proved to be unrealistic, the powerlessness of the Council of Europe was the final proof of this.

So much for the objectives and methods – on this basis, continues Schuman, the French government proposes the following steps::

The entire Franco-German coal and steel production should be placed under a common "High Authority", open for other European countries to join in. This would mean immediately laying the foundations of a common

---

[91] Many witnesses of the time and active colleagues of the directly involved statesmen confirm this hierarchy of priorities, as e.g. the Prime Minister of Luxembourg Joseph Bech, the first of the many Luxembourgers who played an over-proportional role for European integration, compared to the size of his country. Bech said with hindsight in 1966: "What was the real reason why we wanted to create Europe at the dawn of a new day in history after the Second World War? We were convinced that we had to found a new Europe in order to reconcile France and Germany in this new framework. As we see, we succeeded in our fight for a united Europe at least with this important element." Translated from German by HM; quoted from https://www.daskleineeinmale ins.eu/europa/deutschland-in-europa/.

economic evolution, itself the first stage on the way towards a European Federation. This step-by-step approach distinguishes between three separate stages: (1) The "Communitisation" " of coal and steel is (only) the first step, (2) the whole economic evolution the second and (3) the (political) European Federation the third and last stage. In other words: The ambitious goal of the post-war big-bang projects has not been dismissed or abandoned, on the contrary – it should be pursued by a more realistic, more promising method.

After this summary of aims, methods and steps, Schuman focuses again on the overall priority: The "solidarity of production" of both countries, France and Germany, would inevitably " make it plain that any war between France and Germany becomes not only unthinkable, but materially impossible." Then he repeats the succession of the envisaged steps: This solidarity in production should lay the ground for an economic unification of the participating countries.

Several times the horizon opens beyond France and Germany and gains a European scope, other countries are invited to become members and even "the development of the African continent" comes into focus.

And Schuman emphasizes once more that his plan aims at "that fusion of interests which is indispensable for the establishment of a common economic system; it may be the leaven from which may grow a wider and deeper community between countries long opposed to one another by sanguinary divisions" – a further reminder of the peace keeping character of the initiative. Additionally, Schuman affirms that the decisions of the "High Authority" should be binding for France, Germany and the other participating countries, that this would lay the ground for a "concrete foundation of a European federation, indispensable to the preservation of peace."

These, then, are the conditions under which the French government opens negotiations. – after approximately half of the text, the argument starts to become somewhat more technical. What follows is a sketchy description of the tasks to be conferred upon the High Authority on the way towards integration of the markets for coal and steel, i.e. for instance, modernizing production methods, but also harmonizing working conditions – alongside the growth oriented perspective there was also a social one. Additionally, there is a brief foray into transitional stipulations, price policy, customs etc.

Then Schuman turns his eyes to legal and institutional issues: The whole of this field should be enshrined in a treaty. It should comprise an arbitration tribunal (the later European Court of Justice), mandated to survey the implementation of the treaty. The High Authority should be manned by independent personalities, selected by the national governments. There should be a right to object to/appeal against (but not veto) the decisions of the High Authority. A representative of the United Nations Organisation should report twice a year on the new community. Finally, the property of companies should not be limited and the High Commission would have to respect all the rules and competences according to the Occupations Statute, as far as it would apply to the Federal Republic.

The whole text of the speech, printed out, is no longer than two pages (the typewritten version of Mme. Miguez was four pages long), to read it takes no more than ten minutes, if that. The press conference did not last long. Here`s a marginal anecdote: Many textbooks and webpages show photos of Schuman sitting in the Salle d'Horloge at Quai d'Orsay, in front of the crowd of journalists and reading his famous declaration, and there is even a short, barely one-minute-long video, where you can listen to Schuman reading the first sentence of the declaration – but all these photos, as well as the video, are fakes ... or, to put it more mildly, were reenacted later: "Under the haste and stress of the moment, they had forgotten to invite the photographers and the radio broadcasters – so that Schuman had to agree to play the game and read the declaration again, so that posterity would have a visual image to (remember) commemorate the event." Nevertheless, the sensation was perfect. Those over two hundred journalists were perplexed, despite the fact that there had been something of an important diplomatic initiative in the air. One of them asked Schuman, on leaving the room: "But, Minister, this is a leap into the unknown?!" – Schuman's response was sincere: "Yes, you are absolutely right, it is a leap into the unknown."[92] A leap beyond the threshold of national sovereignty,

---

92 Victoria Martín de la Torre has chosen this formula as the title of her book on the founding fathers of European integration: Europe, a Leap into the Unknown. A Journey Back in Time to Meet the Founders of the European Union.

a leap over the threshold of a century old "hereditary enmity" with the Germans – a trial of courage of historical dimensions.

Two hours after Schuman, Adenauer gave his press conference in Bonn. He had let Schuman take the stage first (left the primacy to Schuman), but now it was time for his own interpretation, his own narrative, now it was Adenauer who could take the German public by surprise. It may seem surprising that he first talked at length about the decision of the cabinet to accept the invitation to join the Council of Europe – a controversial decision because at the same time the Saarland, which was then under French administration and not part of the young Federal Republic,[93] was supposed to join the Council of Europe independently. Some in the Federal Republic believed this to signify a definite separation of the Saarland from Germany, and as a sign, albeit implicit, that the Federal Republic officially recognized this step as legitimate. But Adenauer conceived all these things in a wider horizon and pushed for German membership in the Council of Europe(,) because he saw this as a way towards the recognition of the Federal Republic as an equal member of the (Western) family of states, as a way towards a European policy of understanding and mutual trust. In his eyes it was necessary for solving the conflict over the Saarland region, the control of the Ruhr region(,) and the conflict over the Occupation Statute. And the hope that the Council of Europe could still assume the role of an "engine" for the further integration of Europe had not yet totally faded away. For the time being, Adenauer was still convinced that "the aim of the Council of Europe can and must only be this: to create a federal Europe(,)that must become an (entirely) eminently peaceful factor in the world." That is why he urged his audience to "consider and analyse both of these decisions [in favour of the Council of Europe and the Schuman Plan] in the context of mutual interdependence."

Brüssel 2014. The video produced by the Council of the European Union, already quoted, „Europe Through the Generations" (https://www.youtube.com/watch?v=isVdxUBAp78) is based on her book, where Jean-Marie Pelt describes extensively the events around 9th May 1950.

93 Concerning the status of the Saar region at the time see e.g. Rainer Hudemann und Raymond Poidevin (eds.): Die Saar 1945–1955, Ein Problem der europäischen Geschichte. Munich 1999.

Still, he insists on the fact that there was no package deal between the two invitations issued by France: "There were no preceding negotiations, and the decision of the French cabinet [about the Schuman plan] in particular was not an incentive for us to recommend to Parliament [Bundestag] the adoption of the invitation to join the Council of Europe." And Adenauer repeats this chronologically relevant remark after having read Schuman's declaration himself in its entirety: "I want to emphasize again what I said in the beginning, i.e that we did not know anything of this at the moment when we made our proposal [concerning membership in the Council of Europe] in the Bundestag; it was not the French proposal [Schuman's plan] which motivated us to decide upon this recommendation [to join the Council of Europe]." This statement serves as a final contribution to the tricky question of chronology: Adenauer was not among the initiators or close collaborators (,) who elaborated the plan, and the information about Schuman's plan had no impact on the cabinet's decision to join the Council of Europe(,) that same morning – the statement implies that Adenauer at least claims (not only in his memoirs, but in the wake of the turbulent events) that he did not know anything about the Schuman Plan when the decision about the Council of Europe was taken in the cabinet; in other words, Mischlich had not come the day before, but only that same morning. Adenauer talks about an "unexpected event". But, for now, the interdependence between the Council of Europe and the European Community (for coal and steel) is more important than any chronology.

For Adenauer then focusses on Schuman's proposal: "It is certainly of the upmost importance for relations between Germany and France and for the whole of Europe. [...] This initiates, Ladies and Gentlemen, such an eminently important step forward in Franco-German relations that it can hardly be emphasised enough.. " And once again, Adenauer goes into the chronology of events, not without tactical cunning: "Our cabinet has not yet had the opportunity to deliberate on the proposal(,) because it is only this evening that the decision of the French cabinet, taken this morning, has been communicated to the French public. I received the official information about an hour ago." If we take this literally, he is saying that the cabinet has not had a chance to discuss the Schuman Plan – more precisely: the decision of the French cabinet -(,) because the information had come only an hour ago. This is *literally* correct, but the German cabinet could well have been concerned with the proposal, not the decision, that morning. Moreover, the decision of the French cabinet could only be taken after Adenauer's agreement. The reference to the fact that the *decision in Paris* and the information about it came too late for a deliberation in cabinet is nothing more than subterfuge on Adenauer's part, he being fully aware during his own cabinet meeting what was at stake in the French cabinet, taking place at the same time, in the late morning, an excuse for his silence vis-à-vis the German cabinet, and for his single-handed agreement.

Whatever the case, Adenauer binds together the Council of Europe and the Coal and Steel Community under the auspices of a European integration path, heading towards federal unity: "If you read the document [Schuman's plan] again, fully and carefully,, you will find that it refers in many ways to the Europe we all want to shape, to a Federal Europe, and that these two decisions taken today in Bonn and Paris are tightly linked by an organic interdependence."[94]

Jean Monnet sums up the day that evening: "Everything had been made unequivocal within a couple of hours, and was now open to the public, put forward by two men who were courageous enough to bind together the future of their two countries."[95]

---

[94] All quotations from Adenauer's press conference from: https://www.konrad-adenauer.de/quellen/pressekonferenzen/1950-05-09-pressekonferenz.

[95] Monnet, Mémoires, op.cit., pp. 439–441. Monnet mentions the names of some of the journalists representing the most widely read newspapers.

VI After 9th May

10th May ...

The next day Schuman had to advocate his plan face to face with his British and American colleagues. Acheson had been let in on the secret, as we know, but Ernest Bevin, the British Foreign Minister, learned about the plan only after the French government had taken its decision(,) the day before – and was furious. But not only for reasons of communication: The whole approach was the very opposite of what the British had in mind for reshaping the system of European international relations. A supranational bloc(k) on the continent, which would withdraw the state's sovereignty over coal and steel and confer it instead to a supranational authority? That was entirely against the grain, in the eyes of Bevin, since national sovereignty was untouchable, still a tabu for him. And Franco-German cooperation and understanding would be welcome, of course, but not an integrated, united, federal block between the two countries – such a thing would leave no room for the traditional British influence over the one or the other. Of course, the Federal Republic should be integrated into the Western bloc(k), but it should not, together with France – and possibly other European states – go its own way! Acheson had his hands full trying to appease Bevin and to make his, the American approval of Schuman's plan, prevail. However, they were two against one – Acheson and Schuman against Bevin. Even the British refusal could now no longer prevent the plan from being launched and implemented.

And, by the way, not all of the British were opposed to the plan, there was even some sympathy within the diplomatic corps. One week after the conference of the Foreign Ministers, on May 19th, the British ambassador in Paris, Oliver Harvey, wrote an extensive status report and explained how things looked from his own perspective.[96] In this report he not only argues in favour of the coal and steel community as such, but even justifies

---

[96] Letter from ambassador Oliver Harvey to Ernest Bevin, quoted from CVCE: http://www.ena.lu/brief_oliver_harvey_ernest_bevin_pari_19_mai_1950-3-36189.

the secrecy of the plan until the last minute. According to him, Schuman had taken a decisive step towards abandoning the passive, restrictive attitude of France, had switched to an active shaping of the Franco-German relations aiming at peacekeeping, something Bevin and Churchill themselves had urged him to do. The ambassador adds a whole series of further arguments(,) which would have carried some weight, especially in the minds of the British: Once such a European framework was established, Germany would no longer be a threat to France, but it would be closely integrated into the club of the Western powers, a German contribution to the common defense would now be almost unescapable, the danger of a German rapprochement with the Soviet Union – aiming at German reunification, on the basis of neutrality – would be ruled out ... and finally, Harvey even defends the confidentiality of the project, arguing that an earlier public announcement or even a discussion in the cabinet would have watered down the proposal to an extent that would have prevented it from having any real impact, or may have even cancelled it from the French political agenda. But the voice of the ambassador did not count in London – the United Kingdom stood by its refusal. It did not participate in the negotiations over the implementation of the plan, which started at the end of June.

On the way to the European Coal and Steel Community

Italy and the Benelux countries, on the other hand, welcomed the plan wholeheartedly – even if the smaller countries, the Netherlands, Belgium and Luxembourg, were not entirely without misgivings about a Franco-German tandem(,) which had the potential to become an overwhelming force, whereas they themselves might end up as "quantités négligeables", without any influence on "common" policy. These considerations led to requirements concerning decision-making procedures(,) which had to be taken into account during the negotiations. Alcide de Gasperi, Italien Prime Minister from 1945 until 1953, an antifascist Christian democrat() who shared the same values and profound convictions, the same religious fundament with Schuman and Adenauer and who could and did speak German with them, South-Tyrolian as he was, de Gasperi agreed

On the way to the European Coal and Steel Community   101

unreservedly with the plan and pushed for its implementation by any means, regardless of how the institutional setting would look in the end.

What other countries could have taken this first step towards European integration? Ireland, Austria, Switzerland, Sweden and Finland were neutral states and did not or were not allowed (as was the case with Austria) to join any alliance, supranational or otherwise. Denmark and Norway were members of NATO, of course, but ranked their Scandinavian solidarity with Sweden and Finland higher than their attachment to the rest of the continental states; additionally, the close commercial ties Denmark had with the United Kingdom – as much as Ireland – counted too. Portugal, Spain and Greece were under authoritarian rule and therefore did not qualify for a union of democratic states. And Central and (South) East Europe was anyway under the tight grip of Soviet hegemony by now. In the end, there were only the six founding member states: France, the Federal Republic of Germany, Italy, the Netherlands, Belgium and Luxembourg.

The negotiations between "The Six" started at the end of June and dragged on, unlike Monnet had expected, until April of the following year; on April 18th the treaty was finally signed(,) and it took another three quarters of a year before it was ratified and put into force, on ^{t} January 1st 1952. The most tricky issue in the negotiations was the institutional architecture[97] of the future "European Coal and Steel Community", which did not come as a surprise, since it was in this field that the crucial question of power sharing in this innovative, emerging political system had to be resolved: Would it really be an entirely new institution, beyond the nation states[98] and therefore "supra-national"? Or should the member states recapture the power of this institution and place it under their own authority,

---

97 For this paragraph see in particular Hanns Jürgen Küsters: Die Verhandlungen über das institutionelle System der Europäischen Gemeinschaft für Kohle und Stahl. In: Küsters, Die Anfänge des Schuman-Plans, op.cit., pp. 73–102.
98 "Beyond the Nation State" is the title of a book published in 1964 by Ernst B. Haas ((Stanford University Press). Haas was one of the first political scientists who developed a theory of European integration – "neo-functionalism" – in the late 50s, when he wrote a first political scientist's theoretical comment on that strange formation of a new kind of political system emerging on the European continent: The Uniting of Europe: political, social and economic forces, 1950–1957. University of Notre Dame Press 1958.

should they be entitled to issue instructions for it to follow, should the whole system still be more "inter"-national than "supra-"national?

The compromise reached during the negotiations represents a mixture of both options. The smaller member states, the Benelux countries, were most interested in/concerned about maintaining each and every member state, big or small, as a decisive actor and factor in the decision-making procedures, so that the bigger ones, primarily France and Germany, would not pretend to represent "European interests" alone. They successively requested an institution(,) which would represent the member states – more precisely: the ministers in the respective governments charged with coal and steel issues would have some influence on the decisions of the common "High Authority": nothing less than a Council of Ministers.

But then a parliamentary control body was also agreed upon, an assembly of delegates from the national parliaments of the member states. The assembly was not entitled to advise or instruct the High Authority, but it could reverse its power by a vote of no confidence. The Assembly is the forerunner of the European Parliament, which introduced into the institutional system a drive towards parliamentary democracy.

And lastnot least, there was to be a judicial so to speak, constitutional(,) control body, as was already proposed in the original plan with the idea of a court of arbitration. This idea was now turned into a fully-fledged European Court of Justice.

Nevertheless and despite these control mechanisms, the "High Authority" remained dominant and decisive. Later, – when the Treaty of Rome, establishing the European Economic Community and the Euratom Community came into force (in 1958) – it was renamed and transformed into the European Commission. The "High Authority," however, clearly had more decision-making power under the rules of the European Coal and Steel Community than later on and up until today in the European Union.

Admittedly, the whole decision-making capacity of the institutional system, and of the European Coal and Steel Community(,) extended only to these two economic sectors – but that was the very key to its success: The member states only had to sacrifice a seemingly minor part of their sovereignty, only what was needed at the supranational level to ensure peace and create conditions for growth without conflict in the most important fields of industry – enough, on the other hand, to trigger a dynamic of integration(,) which would attract other areas of policy without, however, endangering the readiness of the member states to confer parts of their sovereign rights to the common institutions. That was a delicate balancing act, and would delay the future extension of powers to follow in later, further stages, just as with the geographical expansion of the Community – "deepening", as the extension of competences came to be called, and "widening" (or "enlargement"), i.e. the accession of other states becoming members, these two dynamic concepts were part of the project from the very beginning, nourishing the hope for a common, federal European future.

Part 2 Rethinking the Schuman plan

The story of the Schuman plan has now been told; it could be further extended and deepened of course. Every narrative, every story is selective, it always has limits imposed by the author or circumstances. Those selective limitations can be justified by the content of the story itself, or else for pragmatic reasons, as is the case here ... or would you have bought and read a book with five hundred pages, on "Europe Day" ...? Enough detail for now, then; the events themselves, the question as to who was involved and under what constraints and under which conditions, the profiles of the main actors, all this should be clear enough by now,. But that is not the end of history, of what history can do. It is only now that we can ambulate around the story, so to say, look around it and see it from all sides, all angles, question its meaning, relate the participants to the prevailing circumstances, in other words: It is only now that we can try to *understand* what had happened – this is the moment when the "story" becomes "history". For the events do not always bear their meaning themselves, and it is only their meaningfulness that makes stories worth telling.

The second part of this book asks meaningful questions with regard to the events, questions (,) which can still be addressed/which are still relevant today to the European Union. And this is it what finally makes the story of the events at that time so topical – the "path" towards European integration, chosen in 1950, is still accompanied by the same questions today. And a whole range of questions one may ask of the EU today can only be answered by looking back at the origins of European integration – it is then that the choices were made that still shape the process of European unification. This is the reason why reading and thinking about "Europe Day" is finally not about dealing with "the past", but is another way of making sense of the present situation that is otherwise difficult to understand. The European Union is what it *is* because it has *become* what it is and this emergence started on May 9th 1959 (and in the days before and afterwards).

There are six questions in particular that have been posed from the beginnings of European integration through to the present day, all of them raised with the first step, the foundation of the European Coal and Steel Community, and all of these questions have evoked relevant answers since then:

(I) What was (and is) the relationship between external, extra-European demands, constraints, challenges, and internal, intra-European motivations for integration? Was European Integration borne out of the bloc confrontation, of the Cold War from the outset – or did it, after all, set out to be a peaceful way of solving conflicts between the participating states, France and Germany? Does European integration fit into the narrative of the Bipolar World, or is it a new chapter in the old European story of conflict, war and peace?

(II) Was the European Coal and Steel Community more an economic or primarily a political project? What had priority – recovery, growth, prosperity? … or peace(,) and reconciliation between "hereditary enemies"? What exactly was the relationship between politics and economics, or, more explicitly (since economic policy is politics too, of course), between "low" and "high politics?

(III) A similar question, but with a different focus: Were the tasks conferred upon the European Coal and Steel Community (and its successors, down through to the European Union) tasks rather for managers, pragmatists, technocrats? … or were they intrinsically political, requiring political decisions, not only technical expertise?

(IV) What sort of political system did finally emerge, based on the (Monnet and) Schuman Plan? It was obviously more than an international organization, but less than a state – until then only the one or the other had existed. But what was now at stake seemed to be the fundament for a European "Federation" – did they fulfil this promise/stick to this promise? To what extent?

(V) What was actually the unifying factor among the motives of the participants? Was it the search for a fair balance of interests between France and (West-)Germany, between France and also between the two other Western allies? Was it all about economic and political "interests"? Or was it a common set of values, like respect, reconciliation, peace in a deeper sense? Has the European Union then been launched more as a union of interests or more as a community of values?

(VI) Perhaps the most difficult question, owing to its partly philosophical nature: Were the acting individuals/main protagonists – Monnet, Schuman, Adenauer – bound by structural constraints(,) which in the end dictated the outcome of their actions? Wasn't France obliged to find this or a very similar solution to the German problem(,) simply because the conditions exercised a compulsory influence? Would other individuals, then, have had to act in the same (or a very similar) way? Or was it precisely these personalities, Monnet, Schuman, Adenauer, who did have a choice, who assumed individual responsibility, who make decisions leading to the beginning of European integration?

1 Blocs versus continent? External (extra-European) and intra-European motives for integration

Undoubtedly, there was pressure from the two Anglo-Saxon Western Allies on France to solve the "German problem" in a way which would strengthen the stability and resilience of the Western bloc against perceived or supposed Soviet expansionism. On May 10th and during the ensuing conference of the Western Ministers of Foreign Affairs the French had to deliver such a solution. The formation of the two blocs seemed to be irrevocable in 1950, the world had been divided into two parts, it had become the "Bipolar World".

During the war, President Roosevelt, thanks to the alliance with the Soviet Union against the common enemies – Germany in Europe, Japan in East Asia –, had sketched out a "One World Vision". He believed in the possibility of global cooperation to include both East and West(,) and to this end had launched the foundation of the United Nations Organization. For the sake of this grand design, he had made some concessions regarding the future of Europe. The Bretton Woods conference was meant to lay the ground for a global economic order, *global* in scope, not only for the Western world, which only proved to be the case when the Soviet Union, after participating in the negotiations, then withdrew and did not ratify the agreements. The Marshall Plan, despite being originally offered to the Soviet Union, as well as the Central European states, proved to be a decisive stage on the way to the formation of a separate, Western bloc, when the Soviet Union rejected the American offer and obliged/forced its Central European satellites to do the same. The Berlin Blockade in 1948–49, the putsch in Czechoslovakia in February 1948, and the foundation of NATO the following year were other milestones on the way to the bloc structure.

In 1950 it had become clear that the world would be marked for an unforeseeable future by the antagonism between the two superpowers and their alliances. Europe no longer existed as a whole, as a continent, it was split into an Eastern part, where there was no longer any doubt as to who was in charge – Moscow – and a Western part, more liberal, "free", but which nevertheless had to assume its role in the bloc confrontation. And this applied to all states west of the Iron Curtain, even to the newly founded Federal Republic of Germany. Whether France would like this role or not was secondary. France could prevent the United States, assisted by the United Kingdom, from rearming West Germany and allow for or even actively encourage the renewal of the West German industrial power house, in order to make Germany contribute substantially to the Western defense budget – but only for a limited period of time; in the long run France would have to surrender to the imperative of the bloc logic, that was self-evident in 1950, and this was a threatening perspective/scenario in the eyes of the French.

This conflictual setting had become obvious in 1949, when the Foreign Ministers of the two Anglo-Saxon allies had issued the ultimate demand to their French counterparts to propose a solution to this problem, an ultimatum sympathetic towards French fears, but an ultimatum nevertheless. Indeed, such a perspective would be a challenge, a threat for France(,) and the Americans and the British were fully aware of the problem – that is why they left it to France to find a solution. But France *had* to find and propose one(,) by May 10th 1950 at the latest, otherwise the allies would push their own ideas through and help the West Germans to assume the role assigned to them in the Western bloc, the role France feared so much. Monnet's and Schuman's plan was the response to this challenge – was European integration, then, nothing other than a child of the Cold War, was it driven by the external, bipolar world, by Washington, rather than by the Europeans themselves? And if so, has European integration become obsolete with the end of this global antagonism, after the fall of the Berlin Wall and the end of the bipolar world, since it's "raison d'être" has disappeared?

As plausible as this sounds – there are strong arguments in favour of the opposite, intra-European, internal narrative, arguments for taking into account and even allowing European motives for the launch of a European Coal and Steel Community to prevail. These are primarily concerned with the Franco-German relationship, a relationship of two states both to the west of the Iron Curtain, two states which needed to act on their bilateral relations(,) and not against a third power, the Soviet Union. French fears at the time, as we saw, were less focused on the Soviet Union and its emerging bloc structure than on the "hereditary enemy," Germany, and its potential rebirth as an economic or, even worse, a military power. Should West German industry revive, not only would it annihilate French aspirations to gain access to the West German coal resources for the sake of their own industry, but would also lay the ground for another aggressive arms build-up. For France, the main issue at stake with this launch of a European Coal and Steel Community, was a long term and reliable peace with Germany, and in a way which – contrary to what happened after the First World War – would not again humiliate Germany, which would not again trigger the desire for revenge which had proved to be more disastrous than any attempt to hold their neighbour in check and render the country powerless. When Robert Schuman chose "peace" as the keyword of his speech and ranked it above all other considerations, then he was referring to peace between France and Germany – not between the USA and the USSR; the superpowers and their blocs are not even mentioned in the official declaration by the French foreign minister. Schuman must have been convinced that his exclusively intra-European, initially even bilateral, Franco-German justification of this initiative would be enough to make his approach plausible and legitimate.

Another argument in favour of the intra-European motive is the fact that Schuman places his initiative in a historical perspective, in a European narrative. Facing the world's media, on May 9th he declares that France had been fighting for peace for thirty years – a reference to the Briand memorandum for a European Union in 1930, at the time launched together with and based on an agreement with the then German Foreign Minister Gustav Stresemann. The plan failed, the Nazis came to power ... But Schuman reminds his audience of this initiative and thus focusses on a purely European context, which reaches back long before the emergence of any superpower bloc.

For Schuman personally, the fate of his home region(,) of Lorraine, played a role that should not be underestimated – the suffering of the border regions, which have always suffered the most in all Franco-German wars, is explicitly mentioned in his short declaration. The European Coal and Steel Community and the project of European integration on the whole aimed at keeping peace in these border or trans-border regions, like Lorraine, Alsace, the Saarland and the other neighbouring German regions, as well as Luxembourg, the Southern half of Belgium – all of which were not only coal reservoirs, but, as in Belgium's case, uninvolved victims of nearly all Franco-German conflicts and wars. This subnational, regional dimension of European integration is even further away from the interests of the superpowers than the bilateral, inter-national one.

A similar argument applies to the economic dimension: Jean Monnet started out from an economic point of view, as president of the French economic planning agency. What he had in mind when he drafted the plan was to secure growth for French heavy industry, leading to recovery and a new era of modernization. The plan, which was named after him, the Monnet-Plan, provided a roadmap for accelerated and sustained growth in the French coal and steel industries, and this plan was threatening to fail, since growth had slowed down and was about to stagnate, The limits to this growth in the French coal mines and steelworks had come about – not only due to a lack of resources, but also because of a lack of enterprise and innovation among the managers and owners of those mining and steel-producing companies. Monnet wanted to open up both limitations by opening national borders to gain access to resources(,) and encouraging innovation through transborder competition. Of course he also took into consideration(,) that such a move would at the same time neutralize the conflicts between France and Germany in this crucial field, indeed that it would even make it impossible for Germany to rearm, since the respective resources would be neither under French, nor under German authority – but in future under joint, European, supranational control. And this political perspective was far from being a mere side-effect, it was an equally important, if not overarching political aim. Monnet's arguments, as much as those of Schuman, were convincing without any reference to the bloc confrontation.

Not only during these considerations, officially put forward in public and in parliament, but also at the meetings of the smaller working groups, in the minds of the participating individuals the talks all revolve around the European problem(,) and rarely show any reference to the global one. There is no evidence at any point in time that Jean Monnet, Bernard Clappier, Paul Reuter, Etienne Hirsch, Pierre Uri, Henri Pleven, René Mayer felt they had to bow to any dictate or even request from the Western superpower; the USA and the Soviet Union are simply absent from their

Blocs versus continent? External (extra-European) 113

conceptual planning. This does not mean that Jean Monnet was ignorant with regard to what would happen in London on May 10th(,) when he launched his project; he was surely aware of the burden on the shoulders of the Foreign Minister, of France, and took this factor into account in his plan, worked it out in a way which would make it suitable for solving this problem at the same time. However, _the driving factor behind his and Schuman's ideas was still the internal, intra-European, the Franco-German conflict solution and a peaceful future for both nations, nations at peace with each other.

Jean Monnet considers both aspects, the bloc perspective and the intra-European one, in a "note de réflexion", written down on May 3rd, the day when Bidault had ungraciously criticized him(,) after having been informed about the plan during the cabinet meeting that same morning – Monnet may have found it appropriate to undertake at least one attempt to convince sceptics like Bidault to rethink their position. Monnet's decisive two lines of argument are as follows:

(1) The Cold War threatens to become a real war, one that occupies all political argument, reduces all political thought to a one-dimensional approach, leading to dogged, blind attitudes, prohibiting innovative, creative, alternative solutions – against this blind alley, one must propose actions(,) which free us from the cage of the Cold War and create a new reality(,) which is no longer bound by the antagonism of the superpowers; "Our thoughts focus on one simple and dangerous object: The Cold War. Public opinion considers each and every proposal, every action in the framework of the Cold War. The essential characteristic of the Cold War is to force the adversary to give in and is therefore the first stage of actual warfare (war). This prospect freezes the thoughts of those politically responsible, which is the mark of a strategy aiming exclusively at one single goal. The search for solutions to the problem disappears."[99]

---

99 Jean Monnet, Note de réflexion, 3 mai 1950; the French original reads: „Les esprits se cristallisent sur un objet simple et dangereux: la guerre froide. Toutes les propositions, toutes les actions sont interprétées par l'opinion publique comme une contribution à la guerre froide. La guerre froide, dont l'objectif essentiel est de faire céder l'adversaire, est la première phase de la guerre véritable. Cette perspective crée chez les dirigeants une rigidité de pensée

This does not mean that Jean Monnet's plan for a European Community should be understood as a contribution to the Cold War, but was intended as a breakaway from it, as, an alternative: European integration was not born as a child of the Cold War, but was an attempt to escape from it and its logic.

(2) Germany is emerging once again as a problem for France; if no fundamental solution is found, Monnet anticipates the following scenario: "Germany is already demanding that its [steel] production be increased from 11 to 14 million tonnes. We shall refuse that but the Americans will insist. In the end we will give in, despite our reservations. At the same time French production stagnates or even falls into decline. – We only need to consider these facts and it is quite evident what follows: Germany`s industry expands – leading to German export dumping – there are demands for protection for French industry – leading to the end or dissimulation of the free exchange of goods – the revival of monopolies experienced in the pre-war period – the possible reorientation of German industry towards the East, as a prelude to political understanding – France is back on track towards a limited protectionist production. The decisions leading to such a situation or at least paving the way to it will be taken at the conference in London, under American pressure."[100]

---

caractéristique de la poursuite d'un objet unique. La recherche des solutions des problèmes disparaît." https://www.cvce.eu/obj/note_de_reflexion_de_jean_monnet_3_mai_1950-fr-e8707ce5-dd60-437e-982a-0df9226e648d.html).

100 Ibidem: „Déjà l'Allemagne demande d'augmenter sa production de 11 à 14 millions de tonnes. Nous refuserons, mais les Américains insisteront. Finalement nous ferons des réserves, mais nous céderons. En même temps la production française plafonne ou même baisse. – Il suffit d'énoncer ces faits pour n'avoir pas besoin d'en décrire en grands détails les conséquences: Allemagne en expansion, dumping allemand à l'exportation – demande de protection pour les industries françaises – arrêt ou camouflage de la libération des échanges – recréation des cartels d'avant-guerre – orientation éventuelle de l'expansion allemande vers l'Est, prélude aux accords politiques – France retombée dans l'ornière d'une production limitée protégée. – Les décisions qui vont amener cette situation vont être amorcées sinon prises à la Conférence de Londres sous pression américaine." https://www.cvce.eu/obj/note_de_reflexion_de_jean_monnet_3_mai_1950-fr-e8707ce5-dd60-437e-982a-0df9226e648d.html.

The proposal for a European Coal and Steel Community was meant to prevent this course of events from becoming a reality, to allow for a German economic revival without driving it towards the East, and to impose a similar revival on France, by stripping German competition of its threatening aspects (such as dumping, efficiency, cartels, availability of resources ...). In fact, the Europeanisation of the revival would neutralize and even eliminate the potential for conflict from the very start.

Both arguments, taken together, perfectly reflect the complex relationship between bloc mentality on the one hand and internal European integration motives on the other. It is all about transforming internal European structures in a way which eliminates conflicts between the nation states; bloc mentality is a dangerous distraction from this urgent task. To solve this problem means above all getting rid of this e bloc logic – to become free and creative again, even daring to take a new "leap into the unknown", to initiate a "fundamental change". – "Real unity will not emerge by the simple addition of national sovereignties in councils of any kind"[101], that is Monnet's conviction, nourished by his long experience in this field.

For Konrad Adenauer, too, Franco-German understanding and ideally reconciliation, was both a personal and political wish deeply rooted in his Rhenish culture. For him, this was not simply a secondary function of a turn to the West, which would have been anchored exclusively in the logic of „bloc thinking". European politics, together with France, on the basis of equality was, in his eyes, the ideal project for a peaceful and secure future for the Federal Republic (and in the end for a reunited Germany) in Europe – Adenauer underlines this aspect explicitly in his answer to Schuman (on May 8th or 9th). It is clear that Adenauer was determined to integrate the Federal Republic into NATO, to obtain American guarantees of German security, no doubt fearing Soviet aggression even expecting the outbreak of a Third World War in the near future ... Notwithstanding such fears and to some extent independently from them, (even if in reality his motives were interwoven), his vision for a united Europe aimed above

---

101 Ibidem.: „Ce n'est pas l'addition de souverainetés réunies dans des conseils qui crée une entité."

all at achieving a peaceful understanding and cooperation between the neighbours on both sides of the Rhine, for him self-evident as the Mayor of Cologne, a catholic city with Roman origins bridging the Rhine ... In his eyes, the way towards the recognition of Germany as an equal and trustworthy partner in the European family of nations would inevitably transit through membership of the Council of Europe, as Schuman had proposed, and now, above all, through the formation of a common supranational Community.

And last not least: The ideas about the long term perspectives of Schuman's plan pointed in a decidedly European direction, on both sides of the Rhine. The aim of a European "Federation", with a capital "F", which Schuman had placed at a prominent moment in his speech, had not yet been forgotten, and remained an internal European aim(,) and not a product of the bloc structure. Certainly, the architects of the Marshall Plan – above all, Will Clayton, but also Dean Acheson and George Marshall himself – shared this ultimate goal, but for different reasons. They were mainly interested in strengthening the Western part of the continent(,) so that it would withstand Soviet pressure, and a Federation seemed to be the best means in their eyes to reach this goal; their own American experience appeared to be proof of this. But in the minds of Monnet, Schuman and Adenauer the European Federation was not just meant to fulfil a function for the Western bloc, but it represented first and foremost Europe's own interests, the European institutionalization of the policy of understanding and reconciliation(,) that should prevent war in Europe, should solve conflicts peacefully, i.e. by common law, instead of violence, i.e. war.

What then is the correct description of the relationship between the global bloc mentality and the internal European motives for integration? They were both at work, no doubt. With hindsight and from a long historical perspective, it seems as if the superpowers were the dominating actors(,) who structured world and European politics in the second half of the 20th century and were therefore also initiators of European integration, via pressure on the French to solve the German problem in line with the bloc interests. But with a more detailed insight it becomes obvious that the Europeans, that the French and the Germans had their own bilateral, European agenda, that their motives were more deeply rooted in their history, that these motives were independent and valuable, even without the bloc logic.

So, what of developments since then, and the position today? Again and again, external, often American driving forces, have joined with internal European integration efforts in a way that has sometimes plunged Europe into crises, but has also triggered further steps towards a deepened integration. In this way these extra-European factors have played a role in the configuration of the European political system. The first example of this mechanism occurred very quickly after May 9th, 1950 – when the Korean War broke out(,) on June 25th that same year, the Europeans discovered, with widespread anguish, that they were in the same situation as the Koreans – a potential battleground for open conflict between the superpowers – and that they could easily fall victim to their mutual aggression. West Germany's rearmament seemed now unavoidable, not least because the Americans now needed their troops far away from Europe, in Korea, and would therefore push the West European allies, among them the Federal Republic, to invest more in their own defensive capacities. In October 1950, the French Minister of Defense, Henri Pleven, put forward a proposal for a European Defense Community(,) with a common, integrated European army – which would no longer distinguish, as was the case with the Coal and Steel Community, between French or German, but would only have European troops. It also very quickly became evident that the decision to create such an integrated defense structure meant taking decisions on peace or war together – the most dramatic, existential decision a political community can take, be it a nation or a supranational community. It simply doesn't make sense to launch a defense community without political community, and indeed, the six founding member states of the Community mandated a group of experts and politicians to work out plans for such a political union. The whole project failed in 1954, for reasons which would need too much detailed analysis in this context. But the story shows, despite its failure, that external drivers could trigger the launch, if not the implementation, of internal European projects.

The last example for the time being is the financial, economic and state debt crisis during and after 2008 – triggered in the United States and spilling over into Europe, due to the global interdependence of financial markets. The crisis was not home-made in Europe, but revealed home-made weaknesses and obliged the member states to convene upon laws and treaties(,) which tightened the cohesion among the members of the Monetary Union and the EU as a whole, even if this came at the price of going beyond the Lisbon Treaty, until that point declared to be untouchable. The legal packages, dubbed "Six-Pack" and "Two-Pack", the "rescue funds", several hundred billion € strong (i.e. several times the annual EU budget), the two additional international treaties, which transformed these funds in a sort of European monetary fund (the "European Security Mechanism") and obliged the member states to introduce in their constitutions a brake on debt (that is the "Fiscal Compact") – all these steps towards greater solidarity and tighter mutual control changed the EU without a change in the Lisbon Treaty. In addition, the EU created the "European Fund for Strategic Investment", more than 600 billion € strong, managed by the European Investment Bank, aiming at improving the weak level of investment in the EU member states. Altogether, these measures, funds, laws and treaties raised the level of integration considerably beyond the Lisbon Treaty, convened upon just one year before the crisis broke out, i.e. in 2007, itself still the official constitutional basis for the political system of the EU and proclaimed to fulfil this function for a whole generation. There is no doubt that the balance sheet of European integration after and since 2008 is not entirely positive – the intended solidarity, which materialized in the rescue funds, has fallen victim to mutual accusations and conflict over the conditions under which these funds would be made available; there have also been other crises – none of them triggered in the EU itself, but in their neighbourhood, to the East and South East, from Russia to the Arab World –, and last not least, the decision by the United Kingdom to leave the EU. Still, the EU progresses on its path of integration, if external challenges allow or push for it, forcing the member states to overcome internal resistance, and then internal motivations for deepened integration get their chance, internal motivations(,) which could be reasons enough for pursuing the old aim of federal unification.

II Economics or politics? Was the launch of European integration more an economic move or was it motivated by political objectives?

Coal and steel, two sectors of industry, of the economy – it was economic growth that was at stake, here ... certainly, but only as a secondary factor/priority: The key word, the highest priority between the two hereditary enemies was peace. Both motives are undeniable, but putting the question in the form of economics *or* politics is a trap – the serious way to think about the problem is to look at the specific relationship between both(,) the economy and politics.
First of all, the distinction between the economy and politics must be made clear. M The "Economy", in this context, is of course economic policy: When the European Coal and Steel Community was founded, it was because the participating governments were convinced that these sectors of the economy needed a coordinated, integrated, common *policy* in order to overcome the destruction of the Second World War and to initiate sustained growth. However, the key players were not managers or company owners, but politicians and, as was the case with Jean Monnet, experts. It was all about politics anyway. But what, then, is the difference between "economic policy" and "politics" as such? What it means is finally the distinction introduced by political scientists between "high" and "low politics". Even if the definition of both terms has never been clearly defined and unanimously accepted throughout the scientific community – it is generally recognized that "low politics" comprises all those policies which are not directly concerned with the survival of a nation, of a state, whereas it is the very existence of the nation itself which is at stake in "high politics". "High politics" is then foreign policy, defense and security, the question of peace or war, a choice which is indeed decisive for the

survival of a nation. "Low politics", on the other hand, comprises fields such as the economy or trade.[102]

However, this distinction does not make it any easier to decide whether Monnet's and Schuman's plan was more about "low" or about "high" politics, because the conceptual analysis makes it only more evident that both aspects were, from the very beginning, intrinsically represented in the planning of a European Coal and Steel Community, and not only in the ultimate aim of a European federation. The fact that this was the final goal in the whole process places it in the field of "high politics". The question could still be whether the first step on the path towards "high politics" was deliberately chosen in the field of "low politics", whether the transition to "high politics" was consciously delayed until a later stage of integration.

But a closer look at the events around May 9th does not support this hypothesis of a succession from "low" to "high politics": the latter was involved right from the beginning. Economic development, transborder markets, growth and exchange on the one hand – "low politics" – and international relations, security and peace – "high politics" – were both present in the minds and plans put forward by Monnet and Schuman. That was not a succession, but an integration. Much later, after the failure of the European Defense Community, after de Gaulle had unsuccessfully tried to push the European Economic Community aside and to constrain it to "low politics", when he had proposed a decidedly "high politics" (intergovernmental) *cooperation*, as an alternative, a substitute to (supranational) *integration*, when he failed with this attempt but was still powerful enough to block any advance of the Communities on their way towards deeper integration – after all these experiences, some scholars elaborated the hypothesis that the path towards integration chosen in 1950 may have

---

[102] Robert Owen Keohane and Joseph S. Nye, Power and Interdependence: World Politics in Transition. Boston, 1977. Vgl. auch Stanley Hoffmann: Obstinate or Obsolete? The Fate of the Nation-State and the Case of Western Europe. In: Daedalus, Vol. 95, No. 3, Summer 1966, pp. 862–915. It is here where Hoffmann suggests that Monnet's method works only in „low politics" and argues in favour of his thesis by demonstrating the reasons of the failure of the European Defense Community project and the incompatibility of de Gaulle's "high politics" approach with the community method.

worked well in the field of "low politics", but that it was inappropriate for "high politics", that it would inevitably fail as soon as questions relating to foreign affairs, security or defense policy, as soon as international relations were at stake.[103] But this argument is based on the wrong assumption that Monnet's and Schuman's initiative was exclusively about "low politics" and that "high politics" were not involved. The story told in the first part of this book, the analysis of the sources does not leave any doubt that coal and steel were considered at that time as extremely relevant, as decisive for "high politics", that the European Coal and Steel Community was most definitely about security, peace and the bilateral relations at least between France and Germany, but also in general international relations in Europe as a whole.

The Schuman plan was about economics ("low politics") and ("high") politics at the same time – the remaining question concerns then 'only' the relationship between the two. Logically, there are three conceivable options: (1) Peace and supranational community building were the necessary conditions for growth in the key industries, coal and steel, and the whole of the French and German economies; "high politics" would then be the means to achieve the purpose, this being economic growth and prosperity. (2) The second possibility turns the relationship the opposite way round: The europeanisation of the key industries was the means and the purpose was, in the long run, the emergence of a European Federation. Coal and steel were more or less arbitrarily chosen and could have been replaced by other sectors(,) in order to initiate a transfer of sovereignty which would not be too painful for the participating states. But this hypothesis cannot be confirmed either by the sources or by the story as it unfolded. Nor was "politics" only at the service of economic growth, and the "economy" simply a means for achieving political goals.

A third, more complex possibility is still conceivable and it is this one which can best be applied to the real relationship between economic policy and politics: (3) Shaping the conditions under which coal and steel could grow without international conflict was as much an end in itself as it was a means to achieve political ends, at the service of peace and security, at

---

103 See Keohane, Obstinate or Obsolete, op.cit.

the service of a new type of international relations which was able to avoid the wars of the past. For something – in this case economic policy – to be both an end and a means at the same time is not a logical contradiction/impossibility, and this was indeed the case and what was intended to happen. Moreover, it was this very fact that made Jean Monnet's ideas so ingenious: Those who were sceptical and reluctant vis-à-vis supranational community building could be convinced by the economic argument(,) which was self-sufficient and did not lay claim on the economy for higher ends. As for those who did see the future as a European supranational federation beyond the nation state, one could argue that coal and steel were the best means to start the path towards this final aim.

What is more: The choice of these two sectors of industry was so ingenious(,) because it was precisely these two fields which, more than any others, were bound together and enshrined in "low" and "high politics". On the one hand, these industries were vital for the well-being of the whole of the economies of the industrial states at that time. This was obviously the case with highly industrialized West Germany, but it was also true for the still more agrarian France. It was in these sectors of the economy that recovery and growth was possible, offering a promising path out of the mess the war had left behind, where full employment and prosperity was not an illusion – if politicians were ready to think beyond national borders. At the same time, coal and steel were indispensable at the time (much more so than today) for any form of armament: Nearly all the weapons of the time – tanks, cannons, airplanes, ammunition – could only be produced with coal and steel. If one withdraws the authority over these two industrial sectors from the nation states and confers them to a supranational, European level, then it would be materially impossible for the member states to prepare a war unnoticed, to produce weapons without control, to wage war against each other. That is what Schuman wanted to express(,) when he said that the implementation of his plan would make war between France and Germany "not only unthinkable, but materially impossible".

The European Coal and Steel Community embodied *both elements at the same time*: Economic policy *and* high politics, it aimed at economic growth *and* peace keeping. Economic recovery was of course an aim worthwhile pursuing in itself, fueled by the Europeanisation of the key

Economics or politics? Was the launch of European   123

industries – but at the same time, this communitarisation was, to quote the words of Konrad Adenauer, "The best means to pursue a policy based on mutual trust"[104] and maintaining peace.

And what followed later? And what of the present situation? The question whether the European Union is a group of states aiming at common economic advantages or whether it continues on a path towards European federation, towards a political community in the field of "high politics", is still open – not all the member states, much less all citizens, would give the same answer to this question. It has accompanied European integration throughout its history until the present day. The first attempt to resolve this question and to give a definite answer failed only four years after Robert Schuman's initiative – that was the moment(,) when the French National assembly refused to ratify the treaty for a European Defense Community(,) which would have inevitably lifted the level of integration to federal heights. It took more than a decade before the question arose again: this was in 1965, when the integration process reached the decisive threshold between a customs union and a common market, as envisaged by the Treaty of Rome, establishing the European Economic Community (EEC). But that would have meant the member states accepting common rules, common legislation, and this can only work if everybody gives up the right to veto common decisions, if decisions are taken by the majority. What appears to be more of a technical issue is in fact the crucial divide relating to the challenge of sovereignty: Majority voting means accepting decisions and applying common law, even if you voted against the motion, even if you were in the minority. And then you have given up sovereignty, at least in the policy fields under common rule. It was France once again, in the person of Charles de Gaulle, who was ferociously opposed to such

---

104 Quoted from "Europe Through the Generations", op.cit.. The thesis Keohane and Nye developed much later (in her book: World Politics in Transition, Boston 1977) that "low" and "high" politics had changed their relationship, was already appropriate with regard to the European Coal and Steel Community: „Keohane and Nye describe that previously, the international relations were based on a simple interdependence scheme based on national security: high politics, and that nowadays the international relations are ruled by a complex interdependence based on domestic issues: low politics."

a move, and the Common Market was delayed for a whole generation, until 1992. In 1985 the heads of state and government had finally dared to shrug off the past and agreed upon a new treaty, the "Single European Act", renewing the promise that they would now really implement the Common Market and decide upon the necessary laws by (qualified) majority. At stake this time(,) was global competitiveness, in the first place with the United States, and that could definitely no longer be provided within the narrow national borders. "Low", and "high politics" had merged, as Keohane and Nye had already diagnosed ten years earlier.

The next stage on this path was the Maastricht Treaty in 1992, with Monetary Union, the Euro, as its core policy project. This could be understood as the coronation of economic integration, the solidification of the Common Market by means of a common currency – thus far based on an economic logic (which did not pass uncontested as such). But one could also interpret the Euro as the political glue which would finally bind the Europeans together in an undissolvable union; that was the interpretation of the German chancellor Helmut Kohl. The minting of coins, the introduction of a legal currency, has always been a symbol and proof of the sovereignty of a political system(,) at whatever level – be it local, regional(,) or national. Now this mark of sovereignty was to be allocated at the European level. The Euro was not only a support for the Common Market, it was a symbol of common "high politics".

The introduction of the Euro as a legal currency(,) on January 1st, 1999 (coins and bank notes were only available in 2002) automatically triggered a breathtaking debate: Had European integration reached its final aim, with a Common Market, Monetary Union, and soon the Eastern enlargement, i.e. the reunification of the continent? Was this the integration of "low politics" that had always been envisaged and was now unanimously accepted? /had now been completed? Or were the Common Market, Monetary Union and all other "low policies" always a means towards another end? Weren't they meant to be stages on the way to a "political", i.e. a "high politics" Union? Hadn't the time now come, on the solid basis of economic integration, to reap the harvest, to take that decisive, qualitative leap to the level of a real Federation, just as Robert Schuman had declared half a century ago? That was the European constitutional debate(,) which led in 2003 to the Constitutional Treaty – another attempt that failed because of two negative referenda, in France and in the Netherlands. The reasons for these popular refusals were undoubtedly the internal politics in both countries, but the shock was – Europe-wide – depressing enough to render any attempt to push the treaty through, or to revive the constitutional élan, unthinkable; the formal leap from "low" to "high politics"(,) which had long been a practical reality, was out of reach in constitutional, symbolic terms. The Lisbon Treaty, now in force as the constitutional basis of the European Union, itself the substitute for the abandoned Constitutional Treaty, is in substance (virtually) nothing other than the latter, but disguised in such a way as to make the constitutional dimensions of the treaty unrecognisable.

Under these circumstances, the ambiguity of the EU is still preserved and both interpretations can coexist: The first one considers the EU as an economic community, trusted with only those competences needed to pursue the common economic aims – and the competing second interpretation which views the EU as an "(unachieved) incompleted? federal state", to quote Walter Hallstein, first President of the European Commission, describing it in his political legacy(,) as "an emergent federation" where decisions about the destiny of the member nations and states are taken jointly. This ambiguity of European integration, of the European Union, stems from its birthday on May 9th 1950.

III Management or politics? Was the European Coal and Steel Community a project for pragmatic market management or a genuine political project?

The relationship between the Schuman-Plan and politics can be regarded from another angle(,) that focuses attention on its political dimension in general, both "low" and "high". Already after the First World War(,) a certain mistrust had emerged, not only in this or that state, not only in statehood in general, but in politics as a whole – and as such, politics was held fundamentally responsible for the disasters of the 20th century and came to be considered an inappropriate means to correctly analyse and respond accordingly to the complex problems of contemporary societies and their relationships with each other, at least in the eyes of many thoughtful observers. Politics were, according to this school of thought, far too heavily influenced by archaic modes of perception and behaviour, as, for example, the desire for glory and sovereignty, chimeras of a pre-scientific age. Jean Monnet, despite the fact that he never took notice of theoretical writings, had had exactly this experience in the First World War(,) when he was asked to carry out the pragmatic task of organizing supplies to both the British and French armies, fighting side by side in the North of France; in order to get the necessary information, he had to fight against the secretiveness, the resistance, the national pride of military administrations(,) which simply stood in the way(,) on the grounds of national glory and sovereignty, of finding pragmatic solutions to problems that were obviously common to both – displaying entirely dysfunctional behaviour.

Instead, as the argument went, one could now use and rely on the modern instruments of scientific analysis and problem solving. An age of science had begun, a higher level of civilization, more reasonable than the old atavistic instincts driving "politics". "Technocracy" was the key word, with positive connotations(,) which assigned the capacity of reasonable rule to experts(,). Engineers were the ideal type of science based, scientifically educated, pragmatic, ideology-averse problem solvers. In the United States, a "technocratic movement" was founded soon after the First World War, aiming at the conferral of complex tasks in the economy and society to technicians, engineers(,) and scientific researchers[105], a "Technical Alliance"[106] brought together many engineers(,) who worked, for example, on the self-assigned task of improving the energy supply of the United States.

Solving the contemporary problems of society required not only expertise and knowledge; the complexity, the interdependence, the interconnectedness of those problems had to be analysed and properly understood so that appropriate solutions could be found. Since the 1920s, a genuine branch of technical, biological, social sciences had emerged, focusing on the systemic character of these complex structures and processes, an own approach called "Systems Theory", analysing interconnected and interacting variables, their feed-back cycles, and their behaviour. Ludwig von Bertallanffy, born in 1901, Austrian philosopher and biologist, was one of the pioneers in this new field of system analysis, with a formative impact on early computer science, renamed in this context as "cybernetics": The American mathematician and philosopher Norbert Wiener was a leading representative of this school; in 1948 he published his seminal book on "Cybernetics or Control and Communication in the Animal and the Machine", and two years later "The Human Use of Human Beings – Cybernetics and Society". Five years later David Easton applied the Systems Theory to political science and closed the gap between technocracy and politics, with his epoch-making book "The Political System: An Inquiry into the State of Political Sciences".

David Mitrany, British political scientist of Jewish-Romanian origin, elaborated a comprehensive theory of governance based on expertise and technocratic problem-solving capacity. His reflection on an appropriate system of governance does not start with the unconscious assumption that

---

[105] See e.g. William E. Akin: Technocracy and the American Dream: The Technocrat Movement, 1900–1941. University of California Press, 1977.

[106] See Beverly H. Burris: Technocracy at Work. Albany 1993 und Howard P. Segal: Technological Utopianism in American Culture. Syracuse 1985, 20th anniversary edition 2005.

there are states(,) which are the self-evident primary actors – it starts with the problems which have to be solved and derives from the analysis of the problems an adapted set of capacities, know-how, expertise needed to solve those problems. Experts, scientists, engineers, technicians would be best suited to assume these functions – this being the operative word/ (that is the key word) for the required capabilities. Political institutions, on the other hand, would always mix the pragmatic, goal-oriented solutions with their own internal conflicts and misleading criteria of political success. "Functionalism" is therefore the central concept of this approach, and Mitrany's seminal book, published first in 1943, does indeed claim to solve the biggest problem of mankind by means of technocratic expertise, the problem politicians had just proved they were unable to solve: the title is "A Working Peace System", i.e. a truly functioning, efficient governance system providing peace.[107]

These hopes to solve problems not only via "politics", but via objective, reasonable, science-based expertise both influenced and were in turn influenced by the attempts to achieve scientific economic planning. The Soviet Union claimed to be able to realise such a centralized, top-down, planned economy, and even the market-oriented economy of France was guided and advised by expertise – the French planning agency, the "Commissariat au plan", was inspired by this conviction. Jean Monnet was himself a pragmatic planner and put his hopes on expertise instead of (party) politics; that is the very reason why he was not interested in theories, not even in the one which would best explain his own approach, functionalism. Still, his actions, his behaviour, his convictions fit in perfectly with the functionalist mood of the time.

That is to say, *nearly* perfectly – as we know, he was very close to "high politics" and was conscious that he needed politicians to implement his

---

107 The concept of „functionalism" goes back to a whole epoch in modern culture, when it was widely used in many areas of thought and design – as e.g. in the Bauhaus tradition, where the principle "form follows function" had been shaped, transferred later on European integration, when the theory of (neo-) functionalism dominated the interpretation of the European process. For the origins of the concept see e.g. Susan Lambert: Form Follows Function? Design in the 20th Century. Victoria & Albert Museum, London 1993.

ideas. Monnet needed Schuman if he wanted his plan for a European Coal and Steel Community to become a reality. And Monnet agreed that this new form of supranational governance system needed institutions(,) which could and would not simply deny politics as such, even if they were to be manned by experts – like himself, and he did indeed become the first president of the "High Authority", the precursor of the European Commission. There had to be something like a democratic institutional system, with a two-tier control of its decisions, as in the democratic nation states: one parliamentary control, representing the citizens, and one by an institution, representing the member states, a Council of Ministers; last not least, there had to be an independent, i.e. non-political, legal authority, a court of justice.

The European Coal and Steel Community was then a compromise between politics and technocratic governance: The "High Authority" had the exclusive right of initiative, only this body, with its "technocratic" expertise, could mobilize the whole system; in other words: It could not be put at the service of national prestige or sovereignty policies. Despite the large decision-making competences of the "High Authority", it was subject to the control, in some cases the participation and in extremis even to dismissal by the Council of Ministers and the parliamentary assembly. The hope of the founding fathers was that this model of problem solving, driven by expertise and only accompanied by politicians would prove to be successful, so much so, that other policies would go the same way, that sooner or later this model of governance would become widespread, that it would "spill over", as functionalist theory would put it, to the entire governance system of the member states and that this would in the end lead to a comprehensive, federal union.

That was more than Mitrany had imagined – it was still "functionalism", but with a new, institutional supplement: "Neo-functionalism ctionlism". Ernst B. Haas, American political scientist of Jewish-German origin (born in 1938 in Frankfurt/Main), coined this concept and was one of the first who recognized, in the early years of European integration, a process(,) which seemed to have become an interesting object of study in theoretical terms. In 1958 he published such a reflection on European integration, seen from the angle of neo-functionalist theory, under the title "The Uniting of Europe". His efforts to understand this new phenomenon of governance at a global level and his theoretical reflections culminated six years later with the publication of the benchmark of classical neofunctionalism: "Beyond the Nation State", a provocative title with a more explicit subtitle: "Functionalism and International Organization". Haas' books come very close to a political science theory of what Jean Monnet, the pragmatist, and Robert Schuman, the politician, had launched in May 1950.

And once again: What about today? Is the European Union a technocratic system, as some observers often deplore? *Deplore,* indeed/Deplore being the operative word, because the trust in the capacity of experts to solve the problems of mankind better than politicians has faded away over time. Seventy years of peace(,) and the emergence of the Welfare State have contributed greatly to a revival of trust in the nation state, at least for the first post-war generation. Until the early 70s, the conviction was widespread that science and technology would pave the way towards an ever-improving well-being, towards healthier, longer, easier lives, in peace and security. The European Atomic Energy Community (Euratom)(,) founded in 1958, along with the European Economic Community, is one example of these hopes – the peaceful use of nuclear energy, developed by engineers, pragmatically managed at supranational level – would solve one of the biggest problems of mankind, i.e. providing an abundant energy supply at low cost for everybody. Another such example is the self-confidence of politicians like the German "super-minister" Karl Schiller (so-called because he was responsible for the economy and finance at the same time) He was convinced that he could ensure the "global steering" of economic development in Germany, avoiding recession, based on scientific know-how.[108]

It was not until the crisis of the 70s that this confidence in the problem-solving capacities of science and technology was weakened, when the experts, the engineers of economic growth themselves became exasperated by the inexorable recession, by "stagflation" – i.e. unemployment, due to

---

108 See e.g. Herbert Giersch: Episoden und Lehren der Globalsteuerung. In: Heiko Körner et al.: Wirtschaftspolitik – Wissenschaft und politische Aufgaben. Bern 1976, S. 277–296.

the reduction of economic activity, combined with inflation. At the same time, the Club of Rome came out with the unwelcome message that mankind was about to reach the "Limits of Growth"[109], and that the horizon for these limitations would appear in the near future. "The End of Confidence"[110] also marked the end of the hope Jean Monnet's generation had put on "technocrats" – the concept now acquired negative connotations.

The European Union and the European Commission nevertheless continue to have this Janus-like double face of an institution run partly by technical experts and partly by those with political ambitions. The Commissioners are politicians, nominated by their national governments, but they have to undergo an exam before they can take office: The European Parliament, more specifically the specialized parliamentary committees put every candidate through some tough questioning to test their knowledge. What is required is professional expertise, not political commitment. And it does happen that candidates are rejected, regardless of their political credentials. In general, the European Commission doesn't have all the characteristic features of a political government, not only because it doesn't possess all the competences and decision-making powers of a government, but also because it does not represent the choice of a particular political vision by the European electorate. Again and again there have been attempts to give the European Commission a more political drive, outlook or profile, but on the other hand it has to rely on expertise, since its power is based neither on a clear majority in parliament nor on a stable majority of member states. The Commission is not only obliged to look for the smallest common denominator, but also for convincing solutions to substantial problems. Its emergence from a neo-functionalist era and approach continues to characterize it as an ambiguous, partly technocratic, partly political institution. When Jacques Delors, probably the most influential president in the history of the Commission, called the European Union a "non-identified political object" (referring to the French term for a flying

---

109 Donnella Meadows et al.: Limits to Growth. Potomac Associates, 1972.
110 Konrad Jarausch: Das Ende der Zuversicht? Die siebziger Jahre als Geschichte. Göttingen, 2008.

Management or politics? Was the European Coal and Steel   133

saucer: "object volant non-identifié"[111]), he meant exactly this ambiguity. And this too goes back to its birthday, May 9th 1950.

---

[111] Delors coined this term 9th September 1985 when talking about the "Single European Act", the treaty which definitely launched the Common Market; see https://www.cvce.eu/content/publication/2001/10/19/423d6913-b4e2-4395-9157-fe70b3ca8521/publishable_fr.pdf

IV Federation or international organization? What kind of political system is the European Community/Union?

The question as to whether the European Union, or its predecessor, the European Community, can be identified as a well-known type of political system, or whether it is an entirely new one, a system "sui generis", is fundamental: What sort of system, then, did Monnet and Schuman launch in 1950? – was it an international organization, similar to those already in existence at the time, like the United Nations or the Council of Europe, maybe somewhat better tied together (and limited to coal and steel)? Or was it the early stages of a new type of state, equipped with sovereign rights, entitled to legislate, implement and maybe even enforce the implementation of its laws, superior to national law, aiming at some sort of central government (following the French model), as prefigured in the "High Authority" – the emergence of a "Superstate"?

Or, a third option, should the whole system from the very beginning simulate a federation and develop over time into a fully-fledged federal state, with the well-known horizontal division of power between the legislative, executive and judicial branch, the "High Authority" assuming the role of the executive, of government? The legislative would then be a bicameral system, consisting of the parliamentary assembly, to be elected directly by the European citizens, and the Council of Ministers, representing the member states, as in so many other federations, such as the United States and Switzerland ...? And the Court of Justice would then play the role of a constitutional court, the treaty being the (substitute for a) constitution, laying down the fundamental values and rules for and of the political system? A "government", submitted to democratic control by a bicameral parliament and legal-constitutional control by a court of justice, this setting could invite observers to consider it as the fundament for the European "Federation", the ultimate goal in the process, as announced by Robert Schuman in his speech. This would have been a "multi-layered " system(,) where the member states (and, in federal member states, their regions) would have some competences/decision-making capabilities, whereas other powers would have been conferred on the federal government, at European level. On the whole, the political system could have been identified as a democratic federation, marked by the combination of a horizontal and a vertical division of power.

Jean Monnet had already sketched plans for a European federation during the Second World War, aware of the undeniable fact that the former European "great powers" would be small powers after the war, too small to matter individually in the face of the global power constellation that was emerging. The various different versions of the Monnet-Schuman plan between end of April and May 9th show an ongoing reflection on the issue of the ultimate federal outcome, at first clearly expressed, then clothed in ever more diplomatic terminology, preparing the final text in an effort to stem the ensuing controversy amongst French diplomacy and government members, and perhaps the general public too. The first version suggests a "transfer of sovereignty", a formula which was abandoned in later versions. It openly addressed the need for a "European Federation" and the "necessity to organize Europe on a federal basis". The third version accentuates this approach with a nearly hawkish formula against the nation states' monopoly of sovereignty: "This proposal [...] has a fundamental political meaning: to breach the wall of state sovereignty, sufficiently limited to obtain universal agreement, and sufficiently deep/far reaching as to make the states engage on the path to unity, itself necessary for peace." In a more conciliatory approach, the eight version describes this impetus as the intention to lay down "the first fundaments" of a "European Federation", considered as "indispensable for peace". In Schuman's declaration this formula is further watered down – no doubt this was necessary for it to pass through: His proposal would "lead to the realization of the first concrete foundation of a European federation indispensable to the preservation of peace". After all, the concept of a "Federation" had made it into the final, public version and the previous ones reveal that behind the cautious façade of the openly proclaimed proposal there was a much clearer and committed federal vision which did not back away from the inevitable conflict with the states over the issue of sovereignty. It was revolutionary enough that a French Foreign Minister publicly pronounced the term "federation", all the more so since West Germany was invited to become a member of such a tight and binding form of political community.

Jean Monnet and Robert Schuman had something in common, which might throw some light onto why these two Frenchmen in particular could imagine such a supranational, federal European vision, something which has so far gone unnoticed.: Both of them were outsiders in the Parisian French political milieu, where a Jacobinic, centralistic, sovereignty-oriented political culture had its stronghold. Robert Schuman, as already mentioned, had been educated in a German environment, had absorbed German federal history and culture and felt attached to his home *region*, Lorraine, as much as to the French nation state. A subnational (regional) as well as a supranational (European) federal order was not entirely foreign to his political range of thought. And similarly Jean Monnet: He was born in a region(,) which did not exclusively focus on Paris, but was open to the Atlantic, to overseas, a region which had even fought against Parisian centralism, especially at the time of the French Revolution, when the "Girondistes" around Bordeaux and the insurgents in the Vendée, not far North of Monnet's home region, opposed a federal future for France in favour of the idea that all the sovereignty of the nation should be concentrated in Paris. The French national holiday, July 14th, does not, in reality commemorate the conquest (storming) of the Bastille in 1789, as widely assumed (even in France), but the staging of the "Feast of the Federation", exactly one year after the revolutionary events, a party which united, for a brief moment, the various revolutionary French regions under a common federal umbrella. Monnet and Schuman could, so to say, unfold the federal wings of French political culture and ignite the ever emerging sparks of resistance towards the centralizing, sovereignty-addicted Parisian political culture.

The Germans were particularly delighted by the idea of engaging on a path toward European federation, not surprisingly, since German political history and culture was deeply marked by this model; the only period in German history when a dictatorial centralism prevailed was the twelve-year Nazi regime. During the negotiations on the Schuman plan, the German delegation – its leader Walter Hallstein in particular, together with his close collaborator Carl Ophüls – drafted a plan for a "Coal and Steel Congress." "Congress," in this context, meaning an American-like bicameral parliament: A directly elected parliamentary chamber, a European Parliament, together with a second chamber representing the member states, should in the long run guarantee the federal character of the Coal and Steel Community.

The German parliament backed this intention(,) when it passed a resolution on June 26th 1950 for a European "Federal Pact", insisting on "the conviction that the present fragmentation of Europe in individual sovereign states will inevitably drive the European peoples towards misery and strife" and was therefore "backing a European Federal Pact". This Pact should enshrine a "supranational federal power, legitimated by general, direct and free elections, entitled to assume legislative, executive and judicial power". This federal system should, among other tasks, "initiate the economic unity of Europe on the basis of social justice", should prepare for "a common European foreign policy", should guarantee equality among the peoples of Europe and citizen's rights.[112] "Adenauer's government understood its European policy to be the implementation of this vision into political reality – and it could rely on the widespread agreement and participation of civil society."[113] The German delegation was therefore very well anchored in the negotiations on the Schuman plan and had legal backing in Germany if it wanted to underline and further strengthen the profile of the federal aspects of Schuman's project.

Walter Hallstein, first President of the European Commission between 1958 and 1968, i.e. the man in the driving seat of the newly founded European Economic Community, still insisted in his political testament – a book entitled "The Unfinished Federal State" – on the fact that a fully-fledged federation was still the final goal of European community building, and had been so from the beginning.[114] In the end, the Federal Republic,

---

112 Heinrich Siegler (Hrsg.): Europäische Politische Einigung. Dokumentation von Vorschlägen und Stellungnahmen 1949–1968. Bonn, Wien, Zürich 1968 (= Dokumentation der Deutschen Gesellschaft für Auswärtige Politik), S. 1.
113 Heinrich Schneider: Leitbilder, op.cit., p. 293.
114 Walter Hallstein: Der unvollendete Bundesstaat: europäische Erfahrungen und Erkenntnisse. Düsseldorf 1969; english edition: Europe in the Making. New York, Norton, 1972 See as well Wilfried Loth (ed.): Walter Hallstein. Der vergessene Europäer? Bonn 1995 (Europäische Schriften des Instituts für europäische Politik, Bd. 73).

Federation or international organization? 139

at least around 1950, had nothing to lose – it was not a sovereign state(,) and therefore had no sovereignty to sacrifice, since it was still under occupation ... And to dig a bit deeper: The Nazis had pushed the idea of "nation" to such a nationalistic extreme that they had literally obliterated the idea itself. Why not, then, put all one's hopes on a European federation?

The compromises figured out in the months between June 1950 and April 1951 were decisive for the future development of European Integration, and they allow for all three interpretations of the newly founded political system – that of a centralised system with relatively limited democratic control; that of an intergovernmental system(,) in which the member states cooperate and use common institutions for this purpose; and that of an emerging federal system. The openness of the final goal, criticized time and again since these early days of European integration, the alleged lack of a clearly announced finality, is rooted in these beginnings, and for good reasons: Without these compromises it would never had come into existence, without this openness neither the first nor the steps that followed towards a vaguely formulated "ever closer union" would have been possible. There was never a consensus about any "finality", consensus could only be reached on a step by step basis.

The smaller member states, and above all the Netherlands, but backed by the Belgians, were particularly interested in creating a forum for the individual member states within the institutional system of the new community, mandated to shape decisions(,) on the basis of initiatives launched by the High Authority. This may seem surprising at first glance, since it was precisely the smaller ones who would then appear small in comparison to the big member states – France, Italy, West-Germany. But on the other hand they feared that "European interests", worked out and put forward by the High Authority, assisted by a Parliamentary Assembly, would very much resemble the combined interests of France and Germany, and that they themselves would then be treated as "quantités négligeables". The Benelux countries pushed for an institution to be integrated into the institutional system which was explicitly mandated to channel national interests in the decision-making process – this institution would become the Council of Ministers.

In the end an institutional system emerged, still "sui generis", with a High Authority, entitled exclusively to take the initiative, partially empowered even to make direct decisions, but in most cases bound by an agreement of the Council of Ministers. These decisions were submitted to a control exercised by a Parliamentary Assembly, comprised of delegates from the member states(,) which had no powers to initiate legislation, but could overthrow the High Authority with a vote of no confidence. The European Parliament, first elected directly in 1979, was only given almost equal legislative powers to the Council under the provisions of the Lisbon Treaty in 2007. The negotiators in 1950–51 agreed upon an additional legal control over the functioning of the system(,) in the form of a Court of Justice, similar to a constitutional court in nation states, mandated to watch over the institution and ensure that it acted in accordance with the Treaty.

The Council of Ministers exercised considerable influence over the decisions and increasingly gained more over time, more than the Parliamentary Assembly. The governments had ranked their own interests higher than the interests of those they represented, i.e. citizens and nations, which played a minor role in the Parliamentary Assembly. The citizens had to struggle in a generation-long fight for equality with the governments, and they still did not succeed entirely, since it is now the heads of state and government, meeting in the European Council, who establish the guidelines of European Union policy – an overarching competence they withdrew from the European Parliament (and their own national parliaments) just when it had reached near-equality with the Council of Ministers (today the "Council of the European Union").

And today ...? The list of attempts to clarify and agree upon a final federal plan (federal "finality") has grown long over the decades. Again and again there have been proposals to commit the European integration process, the European Communities, the European Union to the final goal of a European Federation, from the project of a European Constitution, elaborated and voted in with an overwhelming majority by the first directly elected European Parliament in the early 80s, to the attempts to formulate a final federal perspective (federal finality) with the Maastricht Treaty and then, above all, with the Constitutional Treaty, alongside plans and projects emerging in civil society, associations, movements ... such as the speech by German Foreign Minister Joschka Fischer in 2000, on the

Federation or international organization? 141

occasion of the 50th anniversary of the Schuman plan, a speech entitled "From Confederacy to Federation".[115]
A final decision on the final plan for European integration has never been taken. The preamble of the Lisbon Treaty repeats the formula of an "ever closer union among the peoples of Europe", a formula first introduced in the treaties in 1957(,) when the first step beyond the Coal and Steel Community was taken with the foundation of the European Economic Community – a formula wide open to various interpretations(,) because it is not referred to and does not appear in any existing system of political theory, be it federal or confederal, in either centralised or in simply cooperative systems.

The original openness, to put it in positive terms, or ambiguity, a little less positive, remains. The German constitutional court has hammered out its own terminology(,) in its ruling on the Lisbon Treaty and its conformity with the German constitution, and calls the European Union a "Staatenverbund"[116] – a new term, somewhere between confederation and federation, nothing other than a concept for ambiguity, but with one message nevertheless: The European Union, not (yet) being a federation, is more than a confederacy, at best still an "unfinished federal state", as Walter Hallstein said more than fifty years ago, nineteen years after the Schuman

---

115 Joschka Fischer: Vom Staatenverbund zur Föderation – Gedanken über die Finalität der europäischen Integration. "Humboldt-Rede", 12. Mai 2000; english version: From Confederacy to Federation; https://ec.europa.eu/dorie/fileDownload.do?docId=192161&cardId=192161.

116 See the ruling of the German constitutional court on the Lisbon Treaty, 30th June 2009:
https://www.bundesverfassungsgericht.de/SharedDocs/Entscheidungen/DE/2009/06/es20090630_2bve000208.html: „Das Grundgesetzt ermächtigt mit Artikel 23 GG zur Beteiligung und Entwicklung einer als Staatenverbund konzipierten Europäischen Union. Der Begriff des Verbundes erfasst eine enge, auf Dauer angelegte Verbindung souverän bleibender Staaten, die auf vertraglicher Grundlage öffentliche Gewalt ausübt, deren Grundordnung jedoch allein der Verfügung der Mitgliedstaaten unterliegt und in der die Völker – das heißt die staatsangehörigen Bürger – der Mitgliedstaaten die Subjekte demokratischer Legitimation bleiben."

declaration. This ambiguity is another piece of heritage dating back to the birthday of European integration on May 9th 1950.[117]

---

[117] See the four pages long assessment of the scientific service of the German parliament: Vereinigte Staaten von Europa? Verfassungsrechtliche Beurteilung eines europäischen Bundesstaates; 18th January 2018, https://www.bundestag.de/resource/blob/548328/f517c5edcb5bc91843fae0ae3eab9bfa/WD-3-263-17-pdf-data.pdf.

V Interests or values? Was European integration more marked by shared values or was it about balancing interests?

In the middle of the 60s, Hans Peter Ipsen, one of the leading German experts in European law, coined the term "Zweckverband" – an "association of purpose" – for the European Communities on their way towards the Common Market. He looked at the treaties and the competences and tasks conferred upon the European Economic Community, and in particular at those aiming at creating a common market(,) from the angle of international law, taking into consideration the functions conferred to the EEC by the member states *to this purpose*. The ensuing logical characterization of the EEC as a "Zweckverband"[118], an association of purpose, was a highlight in the long discussion(,) as to whether European integration was primarily driven by interest(s) or by (shared) values – Ipsen's contribution was of course an argument favouring the assumption that interests mattered most. If he was right with regard to the comprehensive project of a common market, including the economy as a whole, then the argument should be a fortiori right for the limited sectors of coal and steel? Was the project that Jean Monnet, Robert Schuman, Konrad Adenauer and their colleagues had in mind when they launched their plan, an "association of purpose", aiming at a law-based and therefore peaceful, non-violent balancing of interests? Or was it a project based on common, shared values, at the service of these values, aiming at the emergence of a political entity understood as a community of values?

No doubt interests were involved and did play their role – for the French economy, access to German coal was at stake, Jean Monnet was looking for conditions under which the French coal and steel industries would be fueled towards modernization, by means of transnational competition; Adenauer was equally driven by economic interests, when he wanted the

---

118 Hans Peter Ipsen: Europäisches Gemeinschaftsrecht. Tübingen, Mohr, 1972.

allied restrictions on coal and steel production in the Ruhr region to be lifted; the revival, the recovery of (West-)German industry was at stake for his government; Adenauer tried to neutralize the conflict over the Saarland region, he wanted to re-establish Germany as an equal partner in international relations – all of these considerations fall under the criterion of "interests", and they all did matter in the minds of Monnet, Schuman and Adenauer.

But this was not the whole story, as we know. As it already became obvious when the relationship between "economy" and "(high) politics" was under scrutiny, there was more than recovery and growth in Schuman's mind and plan. However, one cannot simply link interests to the economy and values to politics; there are also interests as work in politics, as the aforementioned German example shows – there is an *interest* in being considered as an equal partner.

The distinction between interests and values is more complex: Obviously, the Schuman plan's political priority was peace-keeping – is peace a value or an interest? The "German Government policy guidelines", e.g., elaborated by the German Foreign Office in 2017, refer to this relationship: "Germany's special responsibility for peace as a result of its history forms the foundation of the guiding principles for peace policy. Preventing wars and genocides, protecting minorities and human rights, are all part of Germany's national ethos. What is more, there are hardly any crises nowadays where the effects are not felt by Germany at some point. Stabilizing crisis-hit countries on a long-term basis is therefore always in Germany's interests."[119] There can be no doubt that peace is as much an interest as it is a value – the distinction may make sense in theory, but in practice interests and values are insolubly interwoven. This is also the case with the initiative to launch a European Coal and Steel Community, an initiative

---

119 The original German version: Auswärtiges Amt: Leitlinien der Bundesregierung: Krisen verhindern, Konflikte bewältigen, Frieden fördern; 17.9.2019; https://www.auswaertiges-amt.de/de/aussenpolitik/themen/krisenpraevention/leitlinien-krisen/217444. the English version two years later, 31st March 2021: Implementation of the German Government policy guidelines: Preventing crises, resolving conflicts, building peace; https://www.auswaertiges-amt.de/en/aussenpolitik/themen/krisenpraevention/-/231878.

driven as much by the desire to secure a long-lasting peace as by the wish to create conditions for economic growth, as much by values like peace, reconciliation, mutual understanding as by the need for economic recovery after the destruction of war.

However, the dimension of values was not limited to peace keeping, it went beyond this and was deeply rooted in the shared convictions and motivations of the politicians involved. One may gradually differentiate between Jean Monnet on the one hand and Robert Schuman on the other, even if this attempt may not be entirely fair vis-à-vis Monnet and his motivation: It seems as if the mixture of interests and values vary in the minds of the two men – after all, Monnet's arguments are more interest-oriented, more concerned with finding solutions to practical economic problems and with European policy, but this is not to deny the existence of values in his projects. Robert Schuman, on the other hand, seems to prioritize values in his political actions, even if he gives no explicit account of the composition of his various motivations. In the absence of reliable sources, there has been much speculation about what could have moved Schuman, during that lonely weekend at home in Scy-Chazelles, between April 28th and May 1st 1950, to launch the U-turn in French policy towards Germany, taking personal responsibility, acting against assumed resistance, proceeding with cunning and political intrigue to implement Monnet's ideas.

It comes as no surprise that the interpretation of Schuman's action relies on his well-known Christian faith, on his intense study of the theology of his time, in particular his proximity to the school of "integral humanism". Against this backdrop, reconciliation, even with "hereditary enemies", is considered a positive value, something honorable, an ethically valuable attitude. And wasn't such a faith in such values indeed what he needed to make Monnet's plan his own affair and realise it? [120] This does not mean in turn that others, on a different basis, could not develop similar sets of values; but in the concrete case of Schuman – and very similar considerations apply to Adenauer – it was just this Christian theology

---

[120] Alan Fimister, quoted already when Schuman's Christian beliefs had to be taken into account, developed this thesis further in his book: Robert Schuman: Neo-Scholastic Humanism and the Reunification of Europe. Brüssel, Peter Lang. 2008.

of reconciliation(,) which provided the fundament of values, capable of bearing the project of a European Community.[121]

Schuman's Christian motivations and his improbable success in applying them to practical politics were even considered as sufficient reason to call for his beatification. An institute was set up in Metz in 1989 specifically for this purpose, the "Institut Saint-Benoît Patron de l'Europe", with no other aim than to promote the beatification of Robert Schuman. To this end, countless documents and other resources have been piled up and transferred to the Vatican(,) in order to support and strengthen this request. On June 19th 2021(,) the Pope finally decided that the decree declaring the beatification of Schuman should be published, as formulated by the official Vatican News. [122] – whatever the official stance of the catholic church may be, it is obvious that Schuman was not exclusively driven by "interests" when he decided to engage with Monnet's plan.

Fifty years after the event ()which forms the basis of this book, on the occasion of this anniversary, Jacques Delors gave a formidable speech in Luxembourg, under the title "Le pardon et la promesse", borrowed from the great Jewish-German-American philosopher in political science Hannah Ahrendt.[123] In his reflection on the "living legacy of Robert Schuman" – the subtitle of the speech – Delors recognizes that the proposal of May 9th 1950 "contained the entire matrix of all that has been realised to date. Everything was there: The significance of the whole enterprise, of course, but also an institutional system(,) which allowed for progress, the so-called 'community method', which is still the benchmark today. Hannah Ahrendt dealt with these topics in 'The Human Condition'(,)

---

121 Catherine Guisan developed this approach into a fully-fledged theory: A Political Theory of Identity in European Integration. Memory and Policies. New York 2012. In this book she draws on the empirical evidence delivered in her former book: Un sens à l'Europe. Paris 2003.
122 Vatican News, 19th July 2021: Robert Schuman, father of European unity, on path to sainthood; https://www.vaticannews.va/en/pope/news/2021-06/robert-schuman-father-of-european-unity-on-path-to-sainthood.html.
123 Jacques Delors: Le pardon et la promesse. L'héritage vivant de Robert Schuman. Speech at the occasion oft he 50th anniversary of the Schuman declaration. Luxemburg, 9th Mai 2000. https://institutdelors.eu/wp-content/uploads/2018/01/discoursv00_01.pdf

much later than the declaration of 9th May. And still, how can one deny the ethical relationship between the two personalities? For the philosopher refers to the gospel to support her thesis. That is why she quotes from the Gospel of Matthew: 'For if you forgive men their trespasses, your heavenly Father will also forgive you.' How could one not link this reference to those Robert Schuman made again and again to this Christian faith? The terms are slightly different, but the spirit is the same: 'Paradoxically, and surprisingly – if we were not, perhaps unconsciously, Christians – we reach out to our enemies of yesterday, not only for reconciliation, but to build the Europe of tomorrow.'"

Hans Peter Ipsen himself recognized much later that European integration, after decades of interest-oriented policies among the "citizens of the market" – another term he coined – had shifted back to the original aim of a value-based community: He now recommended the term "community citizen", a concept which could easily be translated into "citizen of the Union"(,) when the Maastricht Treaty established the "citizenship of the Union" and changed the term "Communities" to "Union". And the Lisbon Treaty, the constitutional basis for the European Union of today, draws "inspiration from the cultural, religious and humanist inheritance of Europe, from which have developed the universal values of the inviolable and inalienable rights of the human being, freedom, democracy, equality and the rule of law"[124] – a literally value-based legitimization of the European Union.

Undoubtedly, there are still today, as always, interests at stake(,) which need to be accepted, promoted(,) and balanced; the European Union is about solving conflicts of interest peacefully, without war, law-based – in the fields of commerce and industry, services and environment, climate, biodiversity, digitalization; it is about preserving European interests at global level, in the WTO, the G20 and other arenas. But at the same time, common values matter, they bind the Europeans together, as clearly spelled out in the Charter of Fundamental Rights of the European Union in

---

124 Lisbon Treaty, consolidated version; see EUR-Lex: https://eur-lex.europa.eu/resource.html?uri=cellar:2bf140bf-a3f8-4ab2-b506-fd71826e6da6.0023.02/DOC_1&format=PDF.

its first sentence: "The peoples of Europe, in creating an ever closer union amongst themselves, are resolved to share a peaceful future, based on common values. Conscious of its spiritual and moral heritage, the Union is founded on the indivisible, universal values of human dignity, freedom, equality and solidarity; it is based on the principles of democracy and the rule of law. It places the individual at the heart of its activities, by establishing the citizenship of the Union and by creating an area of freedom, security and justice.

The Union contributes to the preservation and to the development of these common values while respecting the diversity of the cultures and traditions of the peoples of Europe, as well as the national identities of the Member States and the organisation of their public authorities at national, regional and local levels".[125] This twofold (or 'two-layer') fundament of European integration – association of purpose on the one hand and value-based community on the other – goes back to the plan for a European Coal and Steel Community as proposed on May 9th 1950.

---

125 Charter of Fundamental Rights of the European Union; EUR-lex: https://eur-lex.europa.eu/legal-content/EN/TXT/?uri=CELEX:12012P/TXT.

VI Structures and people "Were structural constraints or the free choice of individuals decisive for the path towards European integration?"

There were many conditions and constraints present at the time which invited and pushed Monnet to develop his plan, Schuman to push it through the French political milieu(,) and Adenauer to accept it on behalf of the (West-)German government. One could tell the story of the foundation of the European Coal and Steel Community without mentioning names, without taking into account the personalities of the politicians involved (,) and the story, told literally impersonally, would still sound plausible, as if everything had been fully explained:

The USA and the United Kingdom, however nuanced their attitudes might have been, were interested in the newly founded Federal Republic assuming its role in the Western Alliance as soon as possible, (faced with) in view of the perceived soviet expansionism. To this end the (West-)German economy was to be allowed to flourish again (particularly in the interests of the British) and the Federal Republic should even be rearmed (to serve the particular interests of the Americans). Both prospects were a problem for France(,) because (West-)Germany could and would then become a threat to French security again – that is why France was invited to solve the problem appropriate to its own interests. For economic reasons it was highly desirable to create an incentive for growth in the French coal and steel sectors, via access to abundant resources (localized in West-Germany) and via transborder competition, revitalizing French entrepreneurs, themselves too passive and not innovative enough.

The formation of the superpower blocs, bilateral Franco-German relations, the economic post-war recovery – all these objective, impersonal, structural conditions pushed towards that which was then actually embarked upon: The Europeanization of coal and steel would bind the Federal Republic tightly to the Western alliance, would provide opportunities for innovation and growth for French companies (and for the Germans too, of course), and would render French fears obsolete. So was the Schuman plan, were Monnet's ideas, Schuman's tactics, Adenauer's agreement, nothing more than that which was due to happen anyway?, Was it simply logical, inevitable and nothing to do with personal genius?, Was it the structural constraints which enforced this solution? More to the point: Was it irrelevant who shaped the plan, who implemented it, who agreed to it? Would others have had to act in a similar way to Monnet, Schuman and Adenauer? Did those involved finally only carry out the executive functions of the structural predicament?

Or was it just the other way round: Was it these very people, these individual personalities who were needed to find a way out of the dilemma, was it down to them with their specific individual profiles, their experience, their convictions, their character? Were they indispensable for making courageous decisions like the transfer of sovereignty to a European Community so that this move toward reconciliation, the "leap into the unknown", "beyond the nation state" could be taken? Could it only have been Monnet, Schuman(,) and Adenauer who were capable of finding imaginative options for a solution(,) which would never have occurred to others? For these three individuals, as we saw, had indeed very specific capabilities(,) which enabled them to find this innovative, revolutionary solution, men who dared to leap into the unknown and envisage a united federal Europe:

Jean Monnet, with his pragmatic analysis of objective factors and who had learned through experience that state sovereignty stood in the way of finding appropriate, pragmatic, functional, output-oriented solutions, who recognised that sovereignty must therefore be ignored, if required; Robert Schuman, with his painful experience shared by so many other Europeans who had been born and had grown up in border regions, victims again and again of the violent conflicts between neighbouring states, with his faith-based convictions that reconciliation, even with a former hereditary enemy, was an honorable, ethically valuable attitude, with his regional identity as a Lorrainer and his supranational, European, Christian identity; Konrad Adenauer, who suffered to the point of physical exhaustion, of mental acrimony, under the fanatism of the Nazis, he who had always felt the cultural proximity and historical ties with the Latin part of Europe, and was therefore wholeheartedly (and not only rationally) convinced that Franco-German reconciliation in a European context would promise a better future, he who shared the same religion with Schuman – was it precisely and exclusively these three personalities who could find the narrow path towards European integration?

As with all previous considerations: putting the question in the form of "either" (structural constraints) – "or" (individual responsibility") would suggest that only one or the other could be true. In reality both elements are, of course, compatible with each other. There was undoubtedly a constellation of structural constraints(,) which objectively demanded a solution, and whoever would have been French Foreign Minister – May 10th 1950 was the deadline for delivering a solution to the question, requested by the two other Western allies about the way in which the Federal Republic could be empowered to assume an active role in their bloc. Nobody would have had the option to deny this constraint, to withdraw without any solution. Jean Monnet could only propose, and Konrad Adenauer could only accept (or refuse); neither of them had either the moral authority (Adenauer on behalf of Germany) or the functional authority (Monnet, without political mandate) to launch and take the decisions required themselves. The French Foreign Minister, and no-one else, was in the driving seat.

But it was not at all self-evident that he would take *this particular* decision, the decision for a supranational Coal and Steel Community. In the field of historical science it is always a pointless exercise, to ask what would have happened if other solutions to the same problem had been at hand. Any attempt to answer such a question is inevitably speculative, since there can be no proof for anything which did not happen. Therefore, it seems very probable that other individuals would have taken other decisions, would have reacted in a different way to the same challenges – in which way is open to speculation. Georges Bidault, for example, was very reluctant vis-à-vis Monnet's plan, as we know. Had he looked deeper into the dossier Monnet had sent to him on Friday, April 28th, had he made it his affair/business – history would have taken a different turn, the European Coal and Steel Community, the necessary path towards European integration, would not have emerged as it did. And had Adenauer not have been elected Chancellor of the Federal Republic(,) on September 15th 1949, with the famous majority of one vote – his own …, – had his social-democratic counterpart, Kurt Schumacher, won the election, then he would probably have refused Schuman's offer. Schumacher was a determined opponent to any Western alliance, bloc, or integration as long as the unity of Germany had not been reconstituted. He wanted to avoid anything which could be an obstacle to German reunification and binding the Federal Republic to Western structures was such an obstacle, in his eyes, whatever its peacekeeping significance may have been. And Jean Monnet – who else could have played the role of an equally ingenious inventor[126]? There had been no other initiative, no ideas, no proposal for solving the problem the other Western allies had put on the French agenda, and most certainly not from the diplomats themselves within the French Foreign Ministry. On the contrary, the plan had to be hidden away from these same diplomats in order that the dominating mantra of sovereignty would not prevent Monnet and Schuman from "breaching the wall of sovereignty".

In short: Others would have acted differently – exactly how differently is, and will always be, an enigma, as is always the case in history, where everything happens only once; the same conditions never occur again in the same way. It was indeed these personalities who were indispensable for finding and implementing this solution to the structural, objective problem, who were able and willing to find and follow this way out of the dilemma, to turn the structural constraints into a promising opportunity. It was their imaginative capacity, their convictions, their courage, their sense of responsibility to take decisions of great historical significance, decisions they took first of all alone, engaging their individual responsibility – later on the democratic institutions of their countries were free to ratify (or not) what they had launched. Monnet, Schuman and Adenauer were not entirely free from any structural constraint, they *had* to act, it was a *predetermined* problem they had to solve, they could not choose the agenda, they *had* to take into account challenges they had not created themselves and which they could not change – but they were free enough to choose this or another path, to assume responsibility or refuse it, to take the decisions or delegate them to others.

---

126 One of his biographers qualifies Jean Monnet as "The inspirator", elevating this capacity to the heart of this personality: Pascal Fontaine: Jean Monnet: L'Inspirateur. Paris, Jacques Grancher. 1988.

"Political leadership" is the term that was coined much later[127] for such an attitude, when politicians, confined by democratic institutions and procedures, assume responsibility and take far reaching decisions on behalf of the common good – the concept has indeed this normative connotation. The phenomenon played a role in the history of European integration at several decisive moments, which then became turning points, for example, in the epoch-making, qualitative, giant leaps towards higher levels of integration in 1985 and 1991: 1985 was the year when the path towards the Common Market was finally agreed upon and promised again(,) in the "Single European Act", negotiated and sealed under a Luxembourg presidency, the treaty which committed the then ten member states, together with Spain and Portugal, joining only a couple of weeks later (1st January 1986), to the final implementation of the core policy project already featured in the Treaty of Rome (?). And this renewal of an old promise, which had not been honoured by political action owing to the resistance of national sovereignty, required a strong political will(,) to work against continued scepticism, required the readiness to assume personal responsibility, required the art of goal-oriented and nevertheless smooth negotiation which had already characterized Robert Schuman's methods. Jacques Delors, President of the Commission, Helmut Kohl, German Chancellor(,) and François Mitterand, President of France, belonged to this historical setting, in the middle of the 80s, the successors of Jean Monnet, Robert Schuman and Konrad Adenauer. And a similar historical situation arose only a couple of years later(,) when the Maastricht Treaty was at stake, with its equally challenging core policy project, Monetary Union. This was designed to irrevocably bind Europeans together demanding another visible and symbolic transfer of sovereignty, when a strong message of European commitment to unification had to be sent to the Central Europeans, who had just got rid of communist dictatorship and were looking for a European future. The same three leaders, Delors, Kohl and Mitterand

---

127 An early discussion of the concept in Léon Dion: The Concept of Political Leadership. An Analysis. In: Canadian Journal of Political Science / Revue canadienne de science politique, Vol. 1, No. 1 (Mar., 1968), pp. 2-17. A classical book on political leadership as a theory of political science is Howard Elcock: Political Leadership. London, Edward Elgar, 2001.

were ready to meet the challenge again and took decisions of historical dimensions. European integration was only ever possible when responsible, forward-thinking, courageous statesmen came together, when "political leadership" was available for the European cause.

However, "political leadership" always had to be collective in order to deliver benefits for Europe – no single national statesmen could pretend to fulfil this role alone; he would always be seen as proponent of the interests of his own country, not as a legitimate representative of Europe. At least two of them were needed to take on the task together – a Frenchman and a German. The Franco-German "tandem" did indeed assume responsibility for Europe on several occasions and at decisive moments, preparing common positions and pushing common decisions through, working together to convince others to agree, often with the support of others, not least from smaller member states, but from Italy too. Those decisions were not clear cut because of the obvious and objective structural constraints that no-one could escape from; these decisions would not have been taken without serious personal engagement.

Conclusions
European integration then and now

When Robert Schuman said in his speech on May 9th 1950 that Europe could not come into existence in one fell swoop, but only gradually, in a succession of small steps, firstly creating a solid basis or "factual solidarity", he was drawing from the consequences of recent experiences: Over the previous five years, just after the end of the Second World War, everything seemed possible(,) because everything was destroyed, nothing was certain – not even statehood, in some parts of Europe. Germany was no longer a state(,) until 1949, and then revived, not as a nation state, but as two states. Even France, so proud of its indivisibility, had to be tied together again(,) after the split into an occupied territory, the Nazi satellite regime with its "capital" in Vichy(,) and an exiled government, first in London, then in Algiers, with collaborators and resistance fighters – split into so many pieces. And Poland, divided from the beginning of the war between Nazi-Germany and the Soviet Union, found itself back on the map in another position, further to the West, losing important parts of its historical territory to the Soviet Union, gaining other territories at the expense of Germany (not yet finalised). The great landmass between the Atlantic and the Soviet Union – France, Germany, Poland – had to recover from the loss of statehood altogether(,) over the post-war years. No surprise, then, that in view of such an all-encompassing challenge, equally far-reaching plans suddenly emerged, that the revolutionary proposal of the "United States of Europe – *now!*" was put forward. And this was not the idea of a few dreamers lacking a sense of realism, on the contrary: None other than Winston Churchill himself spread the vision of such a European Federation(,) following the example of the United States of America. In his famous speech on September 19th 1946 at the university of Zurich, "to the academic youth of Europe", he added: "We must begin *now!*" At the same time, European movements, gathering together in several European countries, held their first international meeting just a few kilometers away(,) and convened upon the "Charter of Hertenstein", birth-document of the "Union of European Federalists" (UEF), enshrining a similar project for a European Federation.[128]

But the big bang projects failed or came to nothing/became bogged down – the Council of Europe, created on May 5th 1949, was the only concrete realization, and even if the Council was initially meant to become the "engine" of further European (federal) integration, it soon became clear that this was not the right approach: to talk about everything (except defense), but decide nothing ... In 1950 there was no longer any way of ignoring the fact that the time for the big bang approach was over. This is what Robert Schuman had in mind(,) when he uttered the sentence quoted earlier. His plan, Jean Monnet's proposal, was the alternative, the result of all this: Instead of a revolutionary leap to create the "United States of Europe", they now proposed a new path – with the same goal! – indeed *path* being the operative word, instead of a one-time leap. The new approach was gradualist, no longer revolutionary. The European Coal and Steel Community was to be the first step, *only* the first step, with others to follow and successively shape a European Community based on the experience of "factual solidarity", and ending up as a "European Federation", as Schuman's text says, a fully-fledged European federal state, just like the "United States".

This was the start of a (hi-)story we call "European integration"[129], a process which was understood as an alternative to a revolutionary, disruptive advance and which would then progress through a series of intermediate stages – a very particular history, the evolution of a new kind of political system, tending towards a federal one, a "Community" or "Union". The fact that this specific history of European Integration occurred is due to the path chosen at its beginning, with all the components discussed in the previous chapters of this book: This history bound

---

128 Listen to Churchill's speech here: https://www.americanrhetoric.com/speeches/winstonchurchillunitedstatesofeurope.htm. The Charter of Hertenstein is still one of the birth documents of European federalism today, e.g. for the British Federal Union: https://federalunion.org.uk/the-hertenstein-programme/.
129 See Schneider, Leitbilder, op.cit., where the author analyses the emergence of the concept of „integration" as just the appropriate term for the method of unification invented and applied by Monnet und Schuman.

interests and values together, economics and politics, pragmatic motives with idealistic ones, reacted to external constraints and pressure, was marked at the same time by internal, intra-European challenges, unfolded its own rhythm of a steadily progressing extension of the Community's competences, a rhythm which would time and again be disturbed, interrupted or accelerated, by conflicts among the member states over the crucial question of how much sovereignty had to be conferred upon the supranational level, disturbed or accelerated by external threats and incentives, put forward by the United States or the Soviet Union, or by decolonization, the dissolution of the European global empires. Most often, the member states have found forward-looking solutions, deepening the degree of integration; but sometimes this has taken several years, and in some cases, has not succeeded at all – anyway, it was never an automatic process, a mechanism, as the (neo-)functionalists of the 50s and early 60s had thought. There was always a need for "political leadership", provided in 1950 by Schuman and Adenauer, together with their colleagues in Italy and the Benelux-countries – Alcide de Gasperi(,) certainly deserves to be mentioned, as well as Paul-Henri Spaak, both of them Prime Ministers of their countries.

Political and social scientists have examined the characteristics and properties of processes(,) that have been launched by an initial decision and put on a specific track, on a "path" – they have worked out whole theories about such a "path dependency", even if they do recognize that there might be moments when the path reaches a crossroad, branches-off, loses orientation and has to change direction/modify its goals.[130]

One such crossroad moment in European integration came in 1977(,) when the Rome Treaties were conceived and launched, laying the ground for the path towards the Common Market, another was when the Maastricht Treaty was agreed upon(,) in 1991,bringing the European Communities into the European Union and launching the Monetary Union, along

---

[130] See the classical theory of „path dependence" in: Douglass C. North: Institutions, Institutional Change and Economic Performance. Cambridge 1990; Paul David: Why Are Institutions the 'Carriers of History'? Path Dependence and the Evolution of Conventions, Organizations, and Institutions. In: Structural Change and Economic Dynamics 5 (1994) 2, pp. 205–220.

with a Common Foreign and Security Policy, and even cooperation in the field of Justice and Home Affairs. In addition, there were the enlargements of the Communities and the Union, starting in 1973(,) with the United Kingdom, Ireland and Denmark joining. But the path leading from the European Coal and Steel Community to the Common Market and Monetary Union and on to the constitution-like Lisbon Treaty was never streamlined or straightforward. Again and again there were big projects, starting with the European Defense Community only a couple of months after the Schuman Plan, the Constitutional Treaty in 2003 – and again and again these big projects failed; again and again the Europeans had to accommodate the smaller, less ambitious, but concrete steps towards a little more integration, with modest substitutes instead of the big projects. Yet it is these substitutes, second best solutions, which have allowed European integration to advance nevertheless – just as Jean Monnet, Robert Schuman and Konrad Adenauer had shown in 1950, when they delayed the realization of the "United States of Europe" for the time being and embarked instead, on what was possible at the time: delivering the first "breach in [the] sovereignty" of the nation states, to implement a first, limited(,) but effective European Community, when they found a "path" that led towards one final aim – a European Federation –, but started with an enforceable and at the same time already revolutionary step. This is the starting point of a story which has changed Europe and continues to do so; seventy years after this initial step, it is still, to quote Wilfried Loth in his seminal book, an "unfinished history".[131]

---

[131] This is the subtitle of the original German edition, the English title is: Building Europe. A History of European Unification, De Gruyter 2015.

www.ingramcontent.com/pod-product-compliance
Lightning Source LLC
Chambersburg PA
CBHW032048300426
44117CB00009B/1234